THE NEW ECONOMICS AND THE OLD ECONOMISTS

The New Economics and the Old Economists

J. RONNIE DAVIS

The Iowa State University Press / Ames, Iowa

J. RONNIE DAVIS is Associate Professor of Economics at the University of Florida, Gainesville. After attending the University of Southern Mississippi (B.S., 1963; M.S., 1964) and the University of Virginia (Ph.D., 1967) and prior to joining the faculty at the University of Florida, he was a member of the economics department at Iowa State University. While at the University of Virginia, he held the Philip Francis du Pont Fellowship, the Thomas Jefferson Center for Studies in Political Economy Fellowship, and the Ford Foundation Doctoral Dissertation Fellowship. His dissertation, out of which this book evolved, was awarded the Tipton R. Snavely Prize, as the best dissertation presented to the economics faculty during the past three years (1966–69). This, his first book-length publication, follows in the wake of a number of journal articles.

© 1971 The Iowa State Universty Press
Ames, Iowa 50010. All rights reserved
Composed and printed by The Iowa State University Press
First edition, 1971
International Standard Book Number: 0–8138–1165–1
Library of Congress Catalog Card Number: 71–126162

TO GORDON AND JIM

CONTENTS

FOREWORD

STRICTLY SPEAKING, this book is a study in the history of economic thought. It is, however, rather different from the normal work in this field. In the first place, it deals with much more recent events than most investigations of the history of economic thought. Further, most investigations of the history of economic thought have dealt with the thought of one economist or a single school. Some have traced the development of a particular theory through time. By contrast, this book deals with the viewpoint of the entire American economics profession during a rather short period of years. The reason for this radical departure from the usual format is simply that this book is devoted to dispelling a myth. Historical myths are, of course, quite common and it is clearly the duty of the historian to dissipate them. Granted the firmness with which the myth attacked in this book is held, it seems doubtful that one book—no matter how well researched—will eliminate it.

The strength of the myth may perhaps be illustrated by the fact that, although I started Dr. Davis on the research which led to this book, I now realize that I was firmly under the control of the myth myself. What little formal training in economics I received was at the University of Chicago. In consequence, I was aware of the fact that the "Chicagoans" had been in favor of fairly drastic expansionary action to prevent or cure the depression very early. I thought, however, that this was an isolated phenomenon—that the whole rest of the profession held the opinions which Keynes attributed to his predecessors. The discovery, as the result of reading Davis's study, that practically *no* leading American economist held these views was a distinct shock to me. I suspect many of the readers of this book will be even more shocked than I was, since they may not be aware (as I was) of the Chicago position in the years before the publication of *The General Theory*.

I must, however, leave the development of the views of American economists on the Great Depression, its causes and possible cures, in the able hands of Davis. After all, he taught me what I know about the subject. Here I should merely like to say a few things about the origin of the myth and about its significance for economics as a profession. In doing so, I shall range outside of the area covered by Davis's book, although perhaps not out of the area which is to be covered by further work. Perhaps my speculations will turn out to be as ill-founded as my views on the subject of this book before Davis did the research herein reported.

It is possibly true that Keynes's remarks about his predecessors aptly delineated the economics profession in England, an area which has not been investigated. It would appear quite likely that they are true about his immediate environment, i.e., Cambridge University. Since Cambridge economists are widely noted for reading only material published by other Cambridge economists, it is even possible that Keynes really thought that the Cambridge point of view was all that counted.

Davis, however, ably demonstrates that the point of view held by almost all leading economists in the United States during the period of the Great Depression was a view which most modern laymen would denominate "Keynesian." Indeed, after reading his book, one wonders where Presidents Hoover and Roosevelt were getting their economic advice. It is certainly true that a number of economists were employed in the Roosevelt administration. Indeed, opponents of the Roosevelt administration very commonly criticized it as being dominated by "crackpot economists." It is clear, however, that neither Hoover —during the great crash—nor Roosevelt—during the agonizingly

slow recovery, interrupted by another major depression in 1937—
were acting in accord with what we can now see was the view
held by the bulk of the foremost economists in the United States.
One is pressed then to discover the reasons why neither president
deferred to the consensus of professional judgment. Indeed, not
only could the depression have been kept to relatively minor
scope by President Hoover, we could surely have recovered
rather quickly if the collective wisdom of the professionals had
only been applied. Instead, we had a catastrophic economic collapse between 1929 and 1933, and then a halting recovery which
might never have reached full employment without the war.
Indeed, the massive increase in the American national product
during World War II was, to a very considerable extent, simply
a recovery from the depression conditions in which we entered
that war.

Granted the overwhelmingly "Keynesian" view of American
economists before the publication of *The General Theory*, it is
not exactly obvious why this book should be held to have been
so influential. Davis demonstrates that there was really very little
new in the book, and what there was that was new was largely
in error. Indeed, most of the reviews of the book by American
economists were unfavorable. This was not because these economists were opposed to the type of measures which are now called
"Keynesian," but because they regarded these measures as old
hat; hence they concentrated their attention in reading the book
upon the technical errors. The fact remains, however, that to
the non-economist and to most economists whose memories do
not extend back into the early 1930s, Keynes is the inventor of
these policy recommendations—a fact that is amply documented
in the widespread use of the word "Keynesian."

It may be that the success of *The General Theory* was largely
the result of the preliminary work done by earlier economists
who had argued for rather similar policies. In a sense, public
opinion is like one of those mountain snow accumulations which
cause so much damage in the Alps. As snow builds up, the likelihood that the whole drift will come crashing down the mountain steadily increases. Finally, the ultimate snowflake falls on
top of the drift, the weight is now too much to be borne, and

the whole drift comes down. Major changes in public opinion tend to take the same form. A very large number of books, articles, and lectures which appear to have no great effect nevertheless prepare the way. Eventually, a critical mass is reached and what appears to be an overnight change of opinion occurs. Perhaps Keynes, coming long after such economists as Fisher and Viner, nevertheless achieved his success largely because of their missionary work.

There are other possible explanations. One which has attracted me, although I must admit I cannot prove it, is that Keynes was engaging in some deliberately dishonest economics with the best of pragmatic motives. If this theory is correct, Keynes had formulated an explanation for Hoover's and Roosevelt's reluctance to follow the advice of economists. He had observed his predecessors arguing that stimulative action should be taken by the government and, at the same time, belaboring various government programs which obviously were aimed at benefiting special interests. Attributing to these interest groups the power to influence government policies, he concluded that it would be possible to get the government to take stimulative actions if the opposition to various specialized programs benefiting special productive groups were changed into advocacy. Thus, a large part of the errors which were seen in his work by his early critics may well have been quite deliberate. At least they are consistent with the hypothesis that he was attempting to obtain political support for ending the depression by appealing to groups which he felt were politically powerful.

Whether he had this idea consciously in mind or not, it must be admitted that one of the effects of the "Keynesian revolution" has been that a number of pressure groups feel less alienated from economics than they used to. Surely this has been one of the reasons for the popularity of vaguely "Keynesian" ideas in the minds of the public. In any event, the Keynesian presentation of those ideas, which had been so widespread among economists, caught on with public opinion and with the politicians, whereas his predecessors had had little or no such effect. For some reason, the public seems to have felt that Keynes was a revolutionary within economics. The view that there were Keynesian economists and non-Keynesian economists, and that the Keynesian economists favored active governmental policies to eliminate depressions, while the anti-Keynesians believed in letting well enough alone, became firmly fixed in popular mythology.

With time, this popular view of the matter became orthodox among economists, too. Perhaps the war, with its practical discontinuance of economic training followed by a great post-war influx, may have accounted for the increasing pervasiveness among economists of a myth once limited to non-economists. Certainly we can find no evidence that American economists at the time Keynes wrote his book saw it as anything other than a presentation of the orthodox opinion, together with some errors. The situation since then has been really most peculiar. If we talk to economists or to noneconomists, we will find that economists can be classified as either "Keynesian" or "non-Keynesian." But the difference between a "Keynesian" economist and a "non-Keynesian" economist when these terms are used by economists substantially deviates from the difference which is attributed to these two words by the general public. The public still thinks of the Keynesian as a man who wants to do something about depressions and the non-Keynesian as a man who is opposed to taking any such action. Oddly enough, there are many non-economists who regard the anti-Keynesian thus defined as being right.

Among economists, however, both the Keynesians and the anti-Keynesians are thought of as interested in action designed to reduce or eliminate depressions. The differences between them are thought to be almost entirely technical. Further, with the accumulation of additional empirical knowledge and improvements in theory, the differences seem to be gradually narrowing.

Thus the public image of the difference between the Keynesian and the non-Keynesian economist is almost totally false. Interestingly, however, certain aspects of the public image seem to be held by the economists themselves. In particular, Keynesian economists frequently seem to feel that such non-Keynesians as Milton Friedman are actually motivated by a feeling that depressions are somehow necessary and maybe even desirable. It is notable, for example, that the Keynesians are critical of Nixon's current anti-inflationary policy which has caused a certain amount of unemployment. The same Keynesians, when Kennedy was in power and followed policies which maintained a very considerable amount of unemployment, remained silent.* The apparent reason for this difference in attitude is a feeling that non-Keynesians might conceivably be in favor of unemployment and, therefore, be deliberately causing it, while the Keynesians must of necessity have been doing their best to eliminate unemployment, and hence the unemployment could not be blamed on them.

Whatever the reasons, the fact remains that there is a major emotional rift in the economic profession which, to a large extent, is not justified. Both the Keynesians and the non-Keynesians are interested in government policies aimed at stimulating growth and preventing or curing depressions. There no doubt are some differences between them in values, but the basic quarrels in the literature are at a technical level. We can anticipate that, with time, they will be resolved. The current level of intellectual heat is very considerably affected by a false idea of the intellectual history of the 1930s. Once we have realized that among economists there was no Keynesian revolution, we will be able to turn our attention to the difficult technical problems and devote less attention to the ideological name-calling.

GORDON TULLOCK

* This is not entirely true of Tobin who did criticize the policy of the Democratic administration *after* he completed his two-year tour on the Council of Economic Advisors. While he was on the Council, however, he appears to have given full support to this policy.

PREFACE

ᘍᘍ IN THIS STUDY I attempted to show that economists representing the classical tradition were more Keynesian in their policy prescriptions than they are commonly credited (or blamed) for being. Leading economists did not favor what has come to be understood as the typical classical prescription—reduction of money wages—but instead took the typically Keynesian position that aggregate demand had to be increased and that the best way to do this was through public expenditures financed by bond issues.

I realize that I have amassed what may seem to some to be an endless series of examples. I feel that this was entirely necessary if a useful *historical reference* on the policy prescriptions of the classical school was to be written. In most cases, I assumed that readers know enough about "Keynes versus the Classics" to recognize for themselves what is remarkable or unusual about statements and arguments. I hope that I have not left too much to the reader. If I have, it is because in writing this book I became perhaps overly concerned with avoiding the style of carping of which I am likely to be accused in any event.

The initial impetus for this work came during early evening bull sessions with Gordon Tullock in the student union on the grounds of the University of Virginia, where I was a graduate student during 1964–67. Everyone who was in Charlottesville during "Camelot" owes a great intellectual debt to Gordon Tullock, but I should like to express my gratitude in particular for his contributions to my intellectual growth and motivation.

I should like also to thank Frank Knight, Jacob Viner, Simeon Leland, and Harry Gideonse for their help. James Buchanan, Leland Yeager, Karl Fox, and Charles Meyer all were of much more assistance in bringing this project to completion than they probably think. I thank each for his patience and encouragement. Finally I should like to express special appreciation to Marcy Haque who not only edited this book but also provided me with a year of intellectual stimulation and challenge in things Apollonian.

THE NEW ECONOMICS AND THE OLD ECONOMISTS

Keynes's Mutiny and the "Old" Economists

⛆ THE PROBLEMS of the late nineteenth and, to some extent, early twentieth centuries were of the sort that generally led U.S. economists to concentrate on resource allocation and economic growth. Little professional attention was devoted to cyclical fluctuations. Nonetheless, economic theory should have led those who studied it at that time to expect cyclical changes as a matter of course. But it did not. Even if economic theory failed to give rise to this perception, the actual recurrence of cyclical aberrations should have mustered an overwhelming interest in stabilization policy. But no such interest appeared. Indeed, it was not until the late 1960s that the situation changed to the extent that economists talk almost as much about stabilization as about the more traditional issues of allocation and distribution. Accompanying this expanded focus are remarkable changes in economic policy and the very study of economics itself. What could have caused such fundamental developments in the outlook of economics?

During the last thirty years many economists and historians have become accustomed to interpreting the phenomenon as the triumph of a single man—John Maynard Keynes—over all his colleagues. Regardless of the importance imputed to Keynes, one thing is indisputable: a change in economic point of view developed out of the Great Depression which successfully challenged the tenets of "financial wisdom." To be sure, the failures of financial traditionalism as remedies of deflation and unemployment were as important in discrediting these mouldy doctrines as the newfledged ideas were in displacing them. The notion of a "Keynesian Revolution," emphasizes the importance of the latter and enshrines Keynes as the key innovator.

Analytical Constructs and Historical Accuracy

At least covertly, sharp distinctions are made between pre-1936, *classical,* and post-1936, *Keynesian* economics. Most of these distinctions derive principally from a reconstruction of classical theory. Most important, the reconstructed classical macroeconomic theory often is shown to differ sharply with the post-1936 tradition, particularly with respect to depression *policy:* it is alleged that the former leads economists to advance contractionary (deflationary) policies, while the Keynesian system leads economists to advance expansionary (inflationary) policies.

Many references to this dichotomy overlook the difference between an *analytical* formulation and a *historical* description. It is no secret that, as an aid to understanding the post-Depression developments and improvements in economics, economists have assembled a body of theory which they denote as "classical." No single economist probably ever held all the ideas comprehended in this reconstructed theory. Although such constructs are analytically useful, it is, as Gardner Ackley has suggested, "historically somewhat inaccurate to talk about (and often to use as whipping boys) the macroeconomic theories of the 'Classical Economists. . . .' "[1]

Despite thirty years of professional discussion and literature devoted to "Keynes versus the Classics," scarcely any of that discourse has systematically tested the historical accuracy of the schism implied by that phrase. The question is, how historically accurate is Keynes's and others' indictment of "classical" econo-

1. Gardner Ackley, *Macroeconomic Theory* (New York: Macmillan Co., 1961), p. 109.

mists? M. Blaug has commented that, "Strangely enough, this
question has not yet been systematically explored."[2]

The Keynesian Revolution

Keynes obviously considered himself to be and wrote as a
revolutionist. And it is understandable that the first wave of his
disciples would emphasize the differences between the "new" economics and the "old." Nowadays, however, economists who are
not writing in the white heat of esoteric quarrel generally agree
that Keynes was far less a revolutionist than often claimed.
"Keynes's assault was directed toward "habitual modes of
thought," a stereotyped cliché-ridden version of received doctrine, and not toward the doctrines representative of the best
exponents of pre-Keynesian analysis.[3]

If it were not for the inaccurate historical inferences which
have been drawn from the "Keynesian Revolution" and
"Keynes versus the Classics" terminology, these phrases would
be harmless expressions of a professional enthusiasm too seldom
manifested by economists, practitioners of the "dismal science."
However, popular misconceptions have arisen from these phrases.
To reiterate, the written and especially the oral tradition commonly designate wage reductions—a sharp contrast to the
"thoroughly Keynesian" cure of government spending and public investment—as the pre-Keynesian economists' prescription for
unemployment. A related convention has been, in effect, to
explain the respective Depression actions of President Hoover
and President Roosevelt partially in terms of the policy advice
given by those wedded to the "old" economics. Presumably, pre-
Keynesians were obsessed with the fetish of an annually balanced
budget, and their recommendations were instrumental in duping
first Hoover and then Roosevelt into pontificating on the necessity of avoiding deficits. The conclusion is that only through

2. M. Blaug, *Economic Theory in Retrospect* (Homewood, Ill.: Richard D.
Irwin, 1968), p. 664.
3. Cf. Axel Leijonhufvud, *On Keynesian Economics and the Economics of
Keynes* (New York: Oxford University Press, 1968).

Keynes's assault on the classical economists was policy successfully oriented away from deflationary tactics and toward effective depression action.

This Study

Two of the tenets underlying Keynes's policy prescriptions for fighting business depression were the usefulness of fiscal policy (especially of public works loan expenditure) and the uselessness of money wage reductions. Keynes advocated these propositions from about 1930 when he presented them in haphazard fashion through 1936 when his more systematic formulation of them, the General Theory[4] was published.

Basically, economists fall into two groups with regard to describing the policy prescriptions of pre-1936 economists (excluding Keynes). The first group carelessly claims that "classical" economists were inveterate advocates of wage cutting as the cure for unemployment and that they failed to support public works expenditures financed by borrowing as well as other expansionary tactics to combat the Depression. The second group, somewhat in the minority, realizes that there were some important exceptions to these generalizations, but, like M. Blaug, they admit that the question of how widespread these exceptions were has gone begging.

To what extent was wage cutting actually embraced in the early 1930s? To what extent were expansionary policies advanced? Have Keynes and the first group above distorted the image of their professional colleagues? Through examination of actual policy discussions and recommendations, this study tries to demonstrate that a large majority of leading U.S. economists affirmed, as did Keynes, the usefulness of fiscal policy and the uselessness of money wage reductions in fighting business depression. Their policy prescriptions were far from being as conservative as people have thought.

4. John Maynard Keynes, The General Theory of Employment, Interest and Money (New York: Harcourt, Brace and World, 1936).

This study cannot attempt the more ambitious task of examining the actual reactions to the Depression by pre-1936 economists in every country. That task must be left to others who perhaps will be encouraged by this study largely of American "classical" economists and their reactions. Even though it is a limited task, however, it is nonetheless tedious, inasmuch as the answers to the questions it raises lie in scores of testimonies before policy makers, reports of commissions, proceedings of round-table conferences, articles and statements in professional and nonprofessional literature, etc.

Some may wrongly interpret this study as an attempt to discredit Keynes and his contributions to economic theory. Little could be further from the truth. Keynes's reputation as an innovator in economic theory is not at stake here. The objection raised is directed solely against Keynes's claim to innovative policy proposals. His original contribution lies not in them but rather in the *theory* with which he supported his policy recommendations. Keynes cannot claim to have converted leading members of the economics profession to his views on policy, for the reason that the profession already held his views (in some cases, before he did). No discipline can long endure the absence of those who are interested in setting its record straight. And if the record is not worth correcting, then that discipline cannot survive the burden of constructing myth upon myth and the disquieting revelation that no one cares.

Probing for Prescriptions

THE NOTIONS of a "Keynesian Revolution" as well as a "Keynes and the Classics" debate have led many to believe that virtually the entire mainstream of pre-1936 economists urged wage reductions and annually balanced budgets as the means of restoring and eventually stabilizing the economy. Taking the "Pre-Keynesian Evolution" point of view, however, one would expect the mainstream of pre-1936 economists to have groped for solutions at the outset of the Great Depression but to have developed more and more reasonable, sophisticated policies as the Depression went along.

By 1930 most U.S. economists probably would have agreed with Keynes in his criticism of Cambridge economics in general and Pigou economics in particular. That tradition had not been developed to deal with short-run fluctuations, and consequently, was not much help in either explaining or understanding the crucial problem during the Depression—nonsecular fluctuations in employment and production.[1] At this time already, poor applications of even the best of classical economics generally attracted little sympathy.[2]

1. Cf. Jacob Viner, "Comment on My 1936 Review of Keynes' General Theory," *Keynes' General Theory: Reports of Three Decades,* ed. Robert Lekachman (New York: St. Martins Press, 1964).
2. Cf. Henry C. Simons, "Keynes Comments on Money," *Christian Century* (22 July 1936), p. 1017.

Policy Discussions and Proposals

A cursory reading of U.S. policy discussion during the early Depression years can be misleading. It may create the impression that these years were characterized almost exclusively by a proliferation of divided opinion. A more careful reading reveals that the consensus on a number of issues of overall policy was simply overshadowed by the heated arguments concerning details. By 1933–35, prevailing opinion had evolved substantially from the pre-1929 distrust of government action in economic matters.[3]

In the United States, existing public policies became the object of close popular and professional scrutiny as the deflation of the 1930s reached unprecedented proportions. Leading economists, sometimes in concert with amateurs, began powerful struggles intended at least to dissuade policy makers from ruinous reactions to the crisis and at best to persuade them to take advantage of the range of sensible policies at their disposal. In part, these concerted efforts served to inform Washington implicitly that economists did possess substantial areas of agreement, in spite of their reputation as a group that could never agree. They were telling the public not to be confused or discouraged by intraprofessional controversy. Together, economists were combating the deflation and its defenders, and, more important, they were confronting directly the popular doctrine that "natural laws" control the economic universe, a doctrine not widely held among American economists and hence not likely to occasion severe controversy among them.[4]

---

3. According to Dorfman, "few knowledgeable persons, including economists, doubted that monetary and credit policy should be revised, that public-works expenditures would have to be extended, and that deficit financing would have to continue" (Joseph Dorfman, *The Economic Mind in American Civilization*, 5 [New York: Viking, 1959], 772).

4. In this regard, Kimmel says that "In early years of the depression, only a small minority of economists held rigidly to the belief that reliance for recovery should be placed solely on the operation of the forces on which the consistency of the classical theory depends" (Lewis H. Kimmel, *Federal Budget and Fiscal Policy, 1789–1958* [Washington, D.C.: Brookings Institution, 1959], p. 205).

IN CONCERT WITH AMATEURS

By the winter of 1930–31 unemployment in the United States had reached startling proportions. At the same time that estimations of relief and construction needs were increasing, it became apparent that yields from normal tax sources would fall short of appropriations. Meanwhile, leaders of groups such as business, religion, and the social sciences were complaining that the administration's request for additional public works appropriations of $150 million was paltry. The stage was then set for the first important public plea for large-scale public construction financed by borrowing.

On 1 December 1930 the Emergency Committee for Public Works, headed by Harold S. Buttenheim of *The American City,* proposed floating a billion dollar "Prosperity Loan." On 5 January 1931 the Committee released a statement bearing the endorsements of fifty-eight mayors and ninety-three economists, including Thomas S. Adams, Thomas Nixon Carver, J. M. Clark, J. R. Commons, Paul H. Douglas, E. S. Furniss, Edwin W. Kemmerer, James E. LeRossignol, Jessica B. Peixotto, Edwin R. A. Seligman, Leo Wolman, and many of the signers of Samuel Joseph's (City College of New York) petition in support of the Wagner Act.

The statement declared that the concerted efforts of business and government had not been sufficient to restore aggregate purchasing power. Its solution to the aggregate demand problem was a billion dollar public works program of expenditures on projects which would not compete with private industry and which could be undertaken immediately.

By the middle of 1931 other notable popular leaders began to attack the fetish of an annually balanced budget. In particular, publisher William Randolph Hearst began to plead for increasing deliberately the national debt to defray a five billion dollar program. In January 1932 Hearst called a conference in New York and was joined in his recommendation by thirty-one "scientific economists" who represented a broad array of academic communities. (See Appendix A, p. 154.) In their report they implied that their policy proposal was neither novel nor inacceptable elsewhere in the profession. For well over a decade, they claimed, economists had been advocating public works construction in periods of depression in order to relieve unemployment and restore purchasing power.[5]

These proposals in 1930 were made at a time when federal construction expenditures were only $230 million, and combined federal, state, and local construction expenditures were less than $3 billion. While the magnitude of these proposals was unrealistic or at least unpractical, they probably served to raise Hoover's construction expenditures in 1931 and 1932.

The resort to petitions seems to have been largely a reflection of the idea that economists must band together and present a united front if their influence was to be maximized. Beyond the Hearst and Buttenheim petitions, there were concerted pleas elsewhere. In April 1931 for example, thirteen economists addressed a telegram to the Federal Reserve Board, asking for an immediate easing of credit. In January 1932 twenty-four economists who participated in the 1932 Harris Foundation Round Tables signed a statement to President Hoover in behalf of a sweeping array of expansionist policies. (See Appendix A, pp. 155–56.) Then in January 1933 more than twenty-five leading economists, including J. M. Clark, George E. Barnett (President of the American Economic Association), and Jacob Viner signed a memorial proposing barter cooperatives for the unemployed.

ECONOMISTS IN THE PUBLIC ARENA

By 1932 almost all news media were publishing commentaries on fiscal policy. Spending was an issue, and arguments for either more or less of it were being stressed by people of opposing persuasions. Economists themselves began to be more and more vocal in public dialogue. In speeches and articles they began to direct themselves to the demands of a nation concerned with lifting itself out of a current crisis and preventing any recurrences of such a catastrophe.

In such statements of the 1920s and early 1930s there seems

5. Cf. Report of 31 Scientific Economists on Programs for Relief of Jobless and Business bv $5,000,000 U.S. Bond Issue. *Congressional Record*, 72nd Cong., 1st sess. 1932, 75, 1655–57.

to have been little doubt among economists that an increase of spending could reduce unemployment in a depression. There was some question, however, as to the means of financing the expenditures in order to achieve the desired effect.

Sumner Slichter, Professor of Business Economics at Harvard University, was particularly outspoken in his criticism of Washington and in his recommendations for recovery and stability. He appeared not the least reluctant to address himself to laymen. In the spring of 1932 for example, Slichter argued in the *New Republic* that the key to America's prosperity was more spending. It did not take a student of economics, Slichter asserted, to understand that prosperity hardly could be regained by spending less and less. On the contrary, he declared, we can restore prosperity only by spending more. In order to stimulate more spending, government would have to take the lead and provide the initial increases, since it was far more able than were most individuals and business enterprises to assume the risk of an increase in expenditures.[6]

Slichter's main point was the illogic of attempting annually to balance a budget which included public works and other capital investments.[7] Policy makers who insisted on balancing such budgets were simply alarmists who, according to Slichter, "by their reckless speeches have fostered a dangerous popular psychology both here and abroad—a psychology which greatly increases the difficulty of shifting to a sensible fiscal policy."[8]

Slichter's arguments were similar to those advanced by Virgil Jordan, tireless economist for the McGraw-Hill Publishing Company. Jordan contended that the need for an expansion of purchasing power under depression conditions made public spending not merely desirable, but necessary. When private spending declined to a low ebb, public spending must be ex-

6. Sumner Slichter, "Should the Budget be Balanced?" *New Republic*, 70, no. 907 (20 April 1932), 262.
7. Slichter's argument was cited time and time again in letters of support (1932) for Senator Wagner's bill (S. 4076). As a matter of fact, Slichter's article was called to the attention of several legislative hearings and was reproduced several times in the *Congressional Record*.
8. Slichter, "Should the Budget be Balanced," pp. 262–64.

panded. "Just as we saved our way into depression, we must squander our way out of it," Jordan argued.[9]

Jordan was convinced in 1932 that no highly developed industrial nation during depression could avoid embracing a policy of public spending as a means of diverting excessive savings into the production of social services.[10] Such expenditures not only increased current capacity to consume the output of the private sector, Jordan said, but they also raised the general standard of living.

It is also noteworthy in passing that Jordan was one of the first economists to anticipate *secular* public spending. He clearly suggested that prolonged deficit budgeting would be necessary to prevent money savings from reducing the income flow necessary for continued prosperity.

Another of the outspoken critics of prevailing budgetary policy was Simeon E. Leland, Professor of Economics at the University of Chicago. In late 1932 Leland expressed concern that the ruinous action which government had undertaken in the name of assisting business out of the doldrums might have the opposite tendency. In particular, Leland feared that the business community, in its attempts to deflate government, might impair the social usefulness of government and thereby injure the very party which was trying to help it. The real crisis of the times, as Leland saw it, represented "a conflict between the social and the individualistic philosophy of government."[11]

Leland's opinion, commonly shared by his colleagues at Chicago (the so-called "Chicago School"), was that public expenditure should be coordinated with business cycles and that no reluctance should be shown toward borrowing to finance such capital outlays. Leland charged that official concern for the annually balanced budget had been responsible for most of

9. Virgil Jordan, address to the 1932 annual banquet of the Pennsylvania State Chamber of Commerce, reprinted in *American City*, 46, no. 6 (June 1932), 51.
10. Ibid.
11. Simeon E. Leland, "How Governments Can Best Meet the Financial Crisis," address to The International City Managers' Association Convention (24 October 1932), *City Manager Yearbook*, 1933, pp. 105–6.

the real and imaginary crises facing governments. "It is erroneously conceived," Leland argued, "that [annually balancing the budget] is the only proper policy year in and year out, regardless of economic conditions."[12] Leland suggested that a wise fiscal policy required a long-term financial program which would take into account the fluctuations of the business cycle and control the policy of the annual budget. In other words, a long-term budget should be balanced over economic periods, and equilibrium between surplus and deficit budgets should be struck over a period of years rather than annually.

Slichter, Jordan, and Leland were typical of economists who operated as activists and popularizers in order to refute the view of an annually balanced budget as a fiscal rule and to secure a new direction for government spending. Through speeches and articles directed toward the intelligent man-on-the-street, they seriously challenged the notion that government economy and higher taxes were the keys to recovery and stability. It would be a mistake to assume that these three economists were alone in the popular arena. There was a diverse array of economists who at the very outset of the Depression began to urge Congress to abandon budgetary balance as an annual rule and to plan instead for a series of deficits.

THE WAGNER BILLS

In January of 1930 Senator Robert F. Wagner of New York reintroduced his bill calling for an Employment Stabilization Board, which would plan public works construction so as to stabilize industry and relieve unemployment.[13] While the bill was being considered, many outstanding economists, including eight past presidents of the American Economic Association and the current editor of the *American Economic Review*, signed petitions of endorsement which later were presented to Congress

12. Ibid., p. 108.
13. The Employment Stabilization Act was first introduced into the Senate in 1928. Philadelphia labor legislation leader, Otto T. Mallery, had inspired the act as a part of a broader government program of stimulating employment.

by Professors Samuel Joseph of the City College of New York and Joseph P. Chamberlain of Columbia University. (See Appendix A, pp. 157–58 for list of signers.) The petition claimed that Wagner's bill was the basis of a national effort to relieve unemployment and that economists widely accepted the use of public works as a means of stimulating construction and employment. Although the Wagner bill passed the Senate without a recorded vote, it was greeted disparagingly with delays in the House. The bill was amended eventually and, in early 1931, passed without appropriations.

It was later—in 1932—that Senator Wagner decided to sample professional opinion on deficit financing. On 20 April of that year, he addressed letters to a number of foremost economists, businessmen, and students of industrial conditions. Senator Wagner's letter read as follows:

My dear sir:

I have introduced in the United States Senate a bill, S. 4076, the principal object of which is to have the Federal Government undertake the construction of its previously authorized public works and to finance such construction by means of a long-term bond issue. The estimated cost of such construction is slightly in excess of $1,000,000,000. . . . My purpose in writing to you is to secure the reaction of an expert, who, by his training, is especially equipped to pass judgment upon this proposal. May I, therefore, ask you to write me freely and candidly?[14]

The responses which Wagner received provided a remarkable symposium on borrowing to finance public works construction as a counterstroke against depression. Wagner did receive opinion which represented dissent and uncertainty in some cases, but the overwhelming weight of opinion favored immediate passage of his S. 4076.

Some Leading Economists. One letter of endorsement came from Frank H. Knight, "Militant Expositor of Neo-Classicism," as Joseph Dorfman called him. Modestly disclaiming expertness

14. U.S., Congress, Senate, *Congressional Record*, 72nd Cong., 1st sess., 1932, 75, pt. 9, 10309. Location of further material quoted from this debate is indicated by page numbers in parentheses following the quote.

and describing himself as a "philosophical economist," Knight claimed that there was an almost universal agreement among economists regarding a deficit budget. "As far as I know," Knight charged, "economists are completely agreed that the Government should spend as much and tax as little as possible, at a time such as this—using the expenditure in the way to do the most good in itself and also to point toward relieving the depression." (p. 10323) Knight suggested that this meant the use of government credit up to the limit of safety.

Morris E. Leeds (Leeds and Northrup Company, Philadelphia, Pa.) also disclaimed expertness in the field. Accordingly, he asked the opinion of Joseph H. Willits (University of Pennsylvania), who in turn deferred to his associate, W. N. Loucks. Loucks pointed out there were several arguments which might be advanced in support of Wagner's bill. "It would seem that one of our greatest needs is for someone to start purchasing something," Loucks began. (p. 10323) Reconstruction had gone in the right direction, he argued, but it had not gone far enough. Making credit more easily obtainable and certain assets more liquid did not really induce borrowing by businessmen. Businessmen borrow, Loucks pointed out, only when they need credit to finance production. If there are no orders to fill, there is no call for production and no demand for credit. The need of the times was for orders and actual purchases. The search for someone to purchase something led rather naturally to the federal government. Consumers were certainly in no position to buy. Their purchasing power had been so widely and deeply cut —they feared even further reductions—that they could not and would not increase their own purchases. The resources of states and cities were practically depleted. A big order, as Loucks called it, could and should come from the federal government, which practically alone had adequate credit to finance it.

From Yellow Springs, Ohio came a carefully considered, lucid argument for expansionary policy by William Leiserson of Antioch College. In arguing for expanded public expenditure and public borrowing, Leiserson also took care to sweep aside the diaphanous arguments to the contrary. Like most others, he claimed to be among the majority of economists. "When you say there is division of opinion as to whether the bill, if enacted into law, would increase employment, tend to stimulate business recovery, promote desirable government activity to take up the slack from private industry and put idle capital to work in a productive manner," Leiserson charged, "you cannot be referring to the opinion of competent and authoritative economists." (p. 10324) Leiserson pointed out that practically all such economists who had studied the question involved favored proposals similar to those included in Wagner's S. 4076. Furthermore, he maintained he knew of no investigating commission considering public works as a remedy for unemployment that had failed to recommend actions similar to those included in Wagner's S. 4076. As evidence, he cited the annual report (1931) of the director of the International Labor Office, which reviewed opinion on public works policy in various countries and strongly endorsed legislation and policy along the lines of Wagner's S. 4076. Also, Leiserson pointed out that countercyclical timing of public works had been advocated by "economists of every school for many years." (p. 10324) He partially based this point on his 1911 report on unemployment for the Wainwright Commission of New York State, in which he found and reported that the prevailing opinion of those who had studied the subject favored countercyclical timing of public works.

Commenting on economic conditions, Leiserson observed that private construction and employment were unlikely to expand without stimulation from expanded public expenditure on public works. Skeptics had only to observe the steady drop in employment and payrolls during the previous two years. In coping with the Depression, private businesses had laid off workers and reduced payrolls, intensifying the Depression which induced these adjustments. As Leiserson saw things, the most important counteracting agent was expanded public expenditure. He was not enthusiastic about the inflation of currency as an alternative.

With regard to borrowing to finance expanded public expenditure, Leiserson argued that there could be no justifiable objection to such a method of financing. The "Treasury View" (as it was known in England) was absurd. On the contrary, the main reason for the present unemployment was that private industry was not in a position to use the available capital.

Leiserson also noted the unsound types of public expenditure which would be ineffective in dealing with the Depression. In particular, he warned against the use of a deficit to help maintain security values. "What is needed," Leiserson argued, "is the use of public credit to provide work and wages, direct purchasing power for the ultimate consumer." (p. 10324)

H. G. Moulton, President of the Brookings Institution, informed Senator Wagner that he had been interested in public works as a depression remedy since the Autumn 1918 publication of his pamphlet, "Public Works or Public Charity." Like some of the others, Moulton admitted he was generally in favor of countercyclical timing of public works. In the present situation, he was definitely in favor of public expenditures, but he feared that a billion dollars would be *insufficient*.

Harvard's Sumner Slichter reiterated to Wagner the persuasive arguments he had made in his recent (20 April 1932) *New Republic* article, "Should the Budget be Balanced?" In that article, Slichter blamed bankers and policy makers in Washington for the reckless talk about the necessity of balancing the budget. Slichter ridiculed the executive and legislative branches for their failure to recognize the problem of recovery as one of aggregate spending. In part, he traced to Washington the roots of a hysterical people who regarded the annually balanced budget as a symbol of the country's soundness.

If the people wanted a balanced budget, Slichter argued, then give them one—all current expenses could be paid out of current receipts. On the other hand, a distinction could be made between current expenses and capital investments. The capital budget would then be financed by bond issues, which would be analogous to private business financing of permanent improvements. When wedded to the countercyclical timing of public works, this proposal for two budgets meant a deficit during depression and a surplus during boom periods.

In his letter to Senator Wagner, Slichter offered practically the same argument. He pointed out that private spending had fallen off dangerously and that "the very process of spending less and less prevents business from getting better and makes it, in many cases, become worse." (p. 10329) Slichter admitted that the Federal Reserve system recently had attempted to stimulate spending by making money easy, but the federal government in its budget was pursuing exactly the opposite policy. This sharp conflict between the Reserve Board's policy and the government's fiscal policy clearly was a serious obstacle to recovery.

Slichter denied that a bond issue to expand public works would divert funds from private industry. He maintained that "the theory that public borrowing would divert funds from private industry overlooks the fact that the money borrowed by the Government would be used to buy goods and hence would increase orders and profits." (p. 10329) A bond issue, therefore, would likely create funds for, rather than divert funds from, private industry.

Frank Taussig, one of Slichter's colleagues at Harvard, also gave his blessings to Wagner's efforts, professing his satisfaction to see Wagner continue his work in behalf of careful and discriminating federal expenditure on public works. Taussig agreed with Wagner that (1) such a program would provide employment directly and indirectly, and (2) a bond issue would not divert funds from private industry. Although Taussig did not see a panacea in deficit-financed public works, he made his position quite clear to Wagner: he was in accord with Wagner that the proper means of financing expanded federal expenditures was the issue of long-term bonds. (p. 10330)

Some Others. Edward Berman (University of Illinois) simply thought that Wagner's proposed deficit was far too conservative. He agreed with Wagner that expenditure on construction and public works definitely would help employment. Since private businesses were unlikely to undertake such projects, Berman thought that the federal government "should undertake the extensive construction of public works." As a hint of the magnitudes he had in mind, Berman pointed out he had been one of the thirty-one economists who had endorsed Hearst's $5 billion bond issue proposal during September 1931. Berman warned Wagner that if the federal government refrained from public-works construction, it would be following "a policy of panic and contraction which is unsound and productive of more intensive depression than that we have so far suffered." (pp. 10310–11) Expansion was the key to recovery, Berman suggested, and the federal government was the only agency with both the opportunity and the stability to expand during times of depression. If government could not be persuaded to expand, the least it could do was refrain from adopting a policy of contraction, Berman argued. Using a war analogy, Berman concluded that people should be at least as willing to use deficits for construction as they were for destruction.

Francis J. Boland (St. Edward's) was one of many who claimed that borrowing to finance construction was a depression treatment on which there was wide agreement among economists. "Your position is economically sound," Boland said, "and . . . your proposed relief remedy is in accordance with the best thought on the matter among economists." (p. 10311)

S. J. Brandenburg (Clark University) feared that some would fail to realize the *multiplier* effects of public works on employment. Senator Wagner had pointed out simply that such a program would provide employment, but Brandenburg wanted it made clear that a program such as Wagner's would also stimulate industries other than those immediately and directly provided for. He pointed out that a public works program financed by borrowing "would stimulate related and contributory industries and would spread outward with diminishing force, to be sure, but ultimately with some degree of benefit to the most remote activities." (p. 10311) Brandenburg also urged Wagner to meet as large a proportion of the cost of public works as possible by borrowing. Even short-term bonds sold in an unfavorable market were preferable to additional tax burdens, he argued. Finally, Brandenburg thought that future use of deficit spending might not meet with official opposition if such a policy were once adopted and carried through.

Walton Hamilton (Yale University) replied to Senator Wagner in favor of countercyclical balancing of the budget and warned him that limiting government expenditures and cutting wages were both antirecovery policies. At the moment, Hamilton complained, there seemed to be too much emphasis on balancing the budget. Hamilton agreed the budget should be balanced over time, but he emphasized that this should be long enough to comprehend the whole of a business cycle. Criticizing prevailing Treasury policy, Hamilton argued against limiting expenditures to amounts which could be easily offset by revenues. Such a practice, Hamilton argued, aggravated the problem of depression. Other official policies were also aggravating the problem of business recovery. Salary cutting of "already underpaid Federal employees," for example, was likely to be followed by private concerns. And if salaries and wages in the private sector were also reduced materially, Hamilton pointed out, public purchasing power would be impaired further. Maintenance of a high level of purchasing power was essential to business recovery, Hamilton claimed.

Earl Dean Howard (Northwestern University) assured Wagner that a deficit would stimulate business and that the injection of the additional funds made available by this means of payment would start prices upward. The English experience provided reassurance that such a policy would not result in a restriction upon international gold payments. Tendencies to hoard gold, in other words, hardly could occur. Lest Wagner think he was speaking alone, Howard told the Senator that the opinion which he expressed was shared by nearly all of his colleagues at Northwestern University.

By this time, many were aware of the multiplier effect which deficit spending should have on spending and income. Henry T. Hunt, for example, suggested to Wagner that the $1 billion expenditure which he proposed would add no less than $10 billion to total purchasing power (implying a marginal propensity to consume of 0.9). The revitalizing effect he anticipated was extensive: "Contractors will purchase from manufacturers who will buy raw materials and engage and pay workmen; the workmen will pay their debts; their creditors will replenish stocks; and industry now on a dead center will be in motion." (p. 10321) Hunt also noted the vast volume of idle capital (cash) seeking investment. This cash simply awaited safe opportunities for investment. Unless the federal government offered such loan opportunities, Hunt argued, billions of dollars would remain hoarded.

William A. Irwin (Washburn College) granted his unequivocal support and expressed his opinion that most economists favored public works as a cyclical stabilizer. In Irwin's opinion, Wagner's proposal of a deficit was undeniably sound from every point of view—economic, social, or other. He pointed out that the types of projects recommended by Wagner would not interfere with private ones, i.e., public construction would not simply take the place of private construction. Private enterprise stood only to benefit by the enhanced purchasing power that would be released. Irwin went so far as to assure Wagner that he knew of no "reputable, socially minded economist" who did not agree that expansionary public works policy was a sound means for dealing with the business cycle.

W. J. Jerome (Linfield College) demonstrated a knowledge of countercyclical budgeting and contributed the notion of a *double* burden associated with unemployment. He proposed that all possible debt should be paid off during times of prosperity in order to provide for a large reserve of credit in depression times with which to keep labor employed in productive work. Unemployment, as Jerome saw it, thrust a double burden on the economy. On the one hand, the product of some five or six million men had been lost. Meanwhile, these men had to be supported in their unproductive idleness.

Although he was not an economist, H. W. Kallen (The New School for Social Research) joined many of the others in claiming a widespread consensus among economists concerning public works and the business cycle. "I agree with practically all the economists of the world," Kallen said, "that public works are an important instrument in flattening out the curve of the cycle." (p. 10323) Kallen admitted that the cycle was not likely to be abolished, but he was convinced along with the others that the difference between peaks and troughs could be reduced considerably.

Ordway Tead, the Business Books Editor of Harper & Brothers, submitted to Wagner a memorandum prepared by members of the Taylor Society, a group active throughout the

Depression in the public arena. The Taylor Society group argued that a primary cause of the Depression was the failure of purchasing power to keep pace with production. In particular, they traced most of the economy's difficulties to a post-1929 glut of capital. As capital became idle, money which otherwise would have been directed to the purchase of goods was rendered unavailable. Demand for manufactured goods and construction decreased sharply, bank and other businesses failed, workers were unemployed, and wages were reduced among those fortunate enough to remain employed—all for the want of purchasing power. Government's reaction to all this was a drastic reduction in expenditures, which further increased unemployment and impaired purchasing power.

The Taylor Society group advanced a rather extensive set of proposals for changes in government and banking policy in hopes of increasing consumer purchasing power and stimulating consumer buying. Its premier recommendation was that government expenditures should be increased largely, thereby employing more men and putting more money into circulation. They argued that this was "the only feasible way to quickly reduce employment and increase purchasing power." (p. 10331)

An Overview. A handful of those responding to Wagner's letter advised against its passage. Notable among the opposition were Johns Hopkins economists, George E. Barnett and Jacob H. Hollander. The former asserted without explanation that "the immediate needs are that Congress should promptly balance the Budget and reject the bonus bill." (p. 10336) Hollander argued, as did Clive Day of Yale University, that Wagner's solution to the problem of unemployment and recovery would be a "menace to our national solvency and to our credit structure." (p. 10338) A. C. Dickinson of the University of Michigan preferred to give large-scale open-market operations further opportunity to work. The University of Minnesota's Alvin H. Hansen, later to have his name most closely associated with the "new economics" of J. M. Keynes, argued simply that it was *not* "an advantageous time to engage in public works on the scale which is suggested in [Wagner's] bill." (p. 10338)

Senator Wagner's sampling of opinion did indeed offer a symposium on depression policy, particularly fiscal policy. If nothing else is obvious, at least it is clear that there was a preponderance of support for Wagner's S. 4076. (For a list of the supporters whose responses have not been cited in the foregoing, see Appendix A, pp. 158–59.) Wage cutting was defended by no one, apparently because reduction of wages was viewed correctly as an impairment of purchasing power. In virtually every case, the argument was advanced that more aggregate spending was the key to recovery and that government was the only agency having the stability and opportunity which expansions of spending during depression required. The idea that a bond-financed expansion of public expenditure would interfere with private projects or divert funds from private employment was denied specifically. The unemployment existed, they argued, because private industry was not in a position to use the available capital.

While there was a remarkable consensus in behalf of bond-financed public expenditure, the *rationales* advanced for deficit budgets during depression were several. In other words, while in agreement on the soundness of deficit financing of an expanded budget, economists in these early years disagreed over the nature and the extent of deficit budgets. The responses to Wagner's inquiry designate three fairly distinguishable schools of opinion: (1) those who argued that countercyclical timing of the "normal" volume of public works was a sufficient stabilization weapon; (2) those who argued for *pump-priming*, a temporary public expenditure program considerably in excess of the normal amount devoted to public works; and (3) those who argued that fiscal policy should be a more or less permanent aspect of stabilization, inasmuch as countercyclical balancing of the budget implies a persistent active role for fiscal policy.

CHICAGO ECONOMISTS: THE PETTENGILL MEMORANDUM

A week earlier than the Wagner letter—on 13 April 1932–Congressman Samuel B. Pettengill of Indiana endeavored to tap the opinions of "the best and most disinterested economic thought of the country with reference to the advisability of either borrowing money or printing money with which to liquidate the adjusted service certificates."[15] This turned out to be the boldest fiscal action of 1931, involving an enactment providing for advance payment, in one swoop, of $1 billion of adjusted service certificates. The passage of this bill by a Congress determined to balance budgets annually was assisted undoubtedly by the fact that all but $100 million came out of a trust fund, which was not included in the administrative budget.

One of the replies he received was in the form of a memorandum endorsed by twelve University of Chicago economists, a group which began to emerge as the most articulate spokesman for a school of thought which advocated (1) the use of deficit budgets as the means of combating depression, and (2) the use of countercyclical balancing of the budget as the means of smoothing out the business cycle.[16]

The Chicago economists argued that severe depression and deflation could be checked and reversed "either by virtue of automatic adjustment, or by deliberate governmental action." (p. 524) They warned, however, that the automatic process involved "tremendous losses, in wastage of productive capacity, and in acute suffering." (p. 524) The Chicagoans did not deny the possibility of recovery by automatic adjustments, but they did deny that it was any less than dreadfully and unnecessarily slow, if politically practicable at all.

In arguing against reliance upon self-healing characteristics of the economy, the twelve Chicago economists conceded that "given drastic deflation of costs and elimination of fixed charges, business will discover opportunities for profitably increasing employment, firms will become anxious to borrow, and banks will

---

15. U.S., Congress, House Committee on Ways and Means, *Hearings, Payment of Adjusted Compensation Certificates,* 72nd Cong., 1st sess., 1932, p. 511. Location of further material quoted from this source is indicated by page numbers in parentheses following the quote.
16. Signers of the memorandum were: Garfield V. Cox, Aaron Director, Paul H. Douglas, Harry D. Gideonse, Frank H. Knight, Harry A. Millis, Lloyd W. Mints, Henry Schultz, Henry C. Simons, Jacob Viner, Chester W. Wright, and Theodore O. Yntema.

be more willing to lend." (p. 524) What undermined the reliance upon automatic responses of the economy was the likelihood that monopolies and public utilities would resist lower prices. As long as wage cutting reduced employment and monopolies resisted lower prices, the Chicagoans argued, deflation might continue indefinitely. Their point was clear. The greater the rigidities of prices and wages, the more drastic the required ultimate readjustment would have to be.

The Chicagoans pointed out that the United States had developed an economy characterized by an exceedingly flexible and sensitive volume and velocity of credit, on the one hand, and by a wage and price system highly resistant to downward pressure, on the other. "This is at once the explanation of our plight," the Chicagoans argued, "and the ground on which governmental action may be justified." (p. 524) Recovery could be brought about "either by reduction of costs to a level consistent with existing commodity prices, or by injecting enough new purchasing power so that much larger production will be profitable at existing costs." (p. 524) Cost reduction, they admitted, would be conveniently automatic, but it also would be dreadfully slow and difficult to facilitate by political measures. Injection of purchasing power, on the other hand, only required a courageous fiscal policy.

The Chicago memorandum implied that recovery was impeded not only by a lack of spending but by a serious price-cost maladjustment as well. The recovery policy favored by the Chicagoans to begin with was an increase of spending, albeit public spending, which would sooner or later cause prices to rise relative to costs. Treating any price-cost maladjustments on the price side had the advantage of reinforcing the recovery mechanism initiated by the public expenditure program.

If recovery were to take place on the price side rather than the cost side, and the Chicagoans said it should, then "it should take the form of generous Federal expenditures, financed without resort to taxes on commodities or transactions." (p. 525) They declined to estimate how much federal expenditure might be required to initiate and bring about a genuine revival of business. They did warn, however, that measures of "fiscal in-

flation" which were too meager or too short-lived were dangerous. "Inadequate, temporary stimulation might well leave conditions worse than it found them," (p. 525) they cautioned, because a temporary, inadequate deficit-financed expenditure might
result in temporary revival and then serious relapse. This was
an obvious attack on the pump-priming version of recovery, i.e.,
the idea that a temporary new expenditure will permanently
raise the level of economic activity.[17]

The Chicago economists were not part of the secular spending school of thought, but they did argue that heavy doses of
stimulant should be used if necessary, continued until recovery
was firmly established, and only then discontinued. In contrast
to the advocates of pump-priming, they recognized a more or less
permanent role for fiscal policy as part of a regimen of compensatory public spending. The pump-priming argument, on
the other hand, ascribed to fiscal policy a temporary role, limited
to a type of "one-shot" injection which was supposed to propel
business back to a stable, full employment equilibrium. Whereas
pump-priming was conceived and supported as a *recovery* measure, compensatory public spending was advocated as a *stabilization* measure.

The Chicago economists found the question of how these
federal expenditures should be financed more difficult and controversial than the question of the expenditures themselves. The
wisest policy, they argued, seemed to be one guided largely by
psychological considerations. The Chicagoans found the issue of
"greenbacks" the most expedient method of financing the public
expenditures, but this method was likely to create the largest
domestic gold drain and to create the most alarm in terms of
public psychology.

A less alarming alternative was the sale of federal bonds in
the open market, but sales to commercial bank and nonbank

17. The Chicagoans' attack on pump-priming came at a time when, according to D. Dillard, Keynes himself "believed in the pump-priming thesis that
temporary injections of government spending would set the wheels of private
enterprise in motion and, once private enterprise was back on its feet, the
government expenditures could be withdrawn without causing any relapse
in total economic activity" (Dillard, *The Economics of John Maynard Keynes*
[Englewood Cliffs, N.J.: Prentice-Hall, 1948], p. 126).

investors had disadvantages in the form of a threat to the prices of such bonds. In light of the encumbrances of issuing green-backs and marketing bonds to the private sector, the Chicago economists argued that the federal government should "sell new issues directly to the reserve banks or, in effect, to exchange bonds for bank deposits and Federal reserve notes." (p. 525) The Chicagoans found much merit in issuing the bonds "with the circulation privilege, thus permitting the reserve banks to issue Federal reserve bank notes in exchange; for this procedure does not much invite suspicion, has supporting precedent, and would greatly reduce the legal requirements with respect to gold." (p. 525)

As one would suspect, the Chicagoans were unconcerned that adequate fiscal inflation might force the United States off gold for a time. "Once a deliberate reflation is undertaken," they argued, "it must be carried through, whatever that policy may mean for gold." (p. 526) If the choice had to be made between recovery and convertibility, in other words, the United States should abandon gold. The Chicagoans cited the English experience as evidence that the departure from gold did not involve the awful consequences often predicted.

As business improved, the Chicago group pointed out, federal reserves would increase automatically. Consistent with the notion of compensatory public spending was the confidence that expenditures would be deficit financed to a lesser and lesser extent as genuine recovery was approached. Inflation, therefore, might be considered the most promising means of restoring a balanced budget. Showing a concern for stabilization as well as recovery, the Chicagoans then argued that Congress should balance expenditures and revenues over a period of time longer than one year, say four or five years. Their point was clear. When wholesale prices and the indexes of production and employment satisfied some norm of aggregate stability, the budget should be balanced; when these indexes suggested a recession, the budget should show a deficit; and when they suggested a boom, the budget should show a surplus. When this series of budgets was put together for the period of a cycle, expenditures and revenues should balance. By and large, their concern was spending: when the private sector is not spending enough, government must compensate for the lack of private spending in the form of new government spending, financed preferably by the sale of bonds to reserve banks; when the private sector is spending too much, government must compensate for this excess spending in the form of reduced government spending and/or increased taxes, the surplus being disposed of by the retirement of reserve-owned bonds (which, if supported by restrictive reserve policy, reduces the stock of money).

A comprehensive appraisal of depression and stabilization policy, the Chicago economists' memorandum to Congressman Pettengill was an articulate statement sharply in contrast to some modern descriptions of classical economists. They did admit that, given drastic deflation, the self-healing or automatic adjustments of the economy could bring about recovery. What they denied was that wage cutting and price cutting could bring about recovery without unnecessary losses of output, wastage of capacity, and suffering in general. It was obvious to them that the road to recovery was not paved with deflation, but rather with public spending financed by "public credit."

When combined with other Chicago documents, the Pettengill memorandum makes it clear that this group of "classical" economists was among the earliest spokesmen for the simple truths of compensatory public finance. The Chicago economics argued strongly for a fiscal stabilization policy which, during recovery, called for large, continuous government expenditures financed by the sale of bonds to reserve banks (a modern version of printing money) and which, during boom, called for smaller levels of spending and a surplus budget disposed of by retiring reserve-held debt.

Hoover and Roosevelt: Executive Reactions

For at least a decade, Herbert Hoover had believed in the long-range planning and countercyclical timing of public works construction. In 1923 for example, then Secretary of Commerce Hoover endorsed the findings and recommendations of

the President's Conference on Unemployment. In the Foreword
to this report he summed up and agreed with the Conference's
suggestions "as to the deferment of public work and construction work of large public-service corporations to periods of depression and unemployment, which, while in the nature of relief
from evils already created, would tend both by their subtraction
from production at the peak of the boom and addition of production in the valley of depression toward more even progress
of business itself."[18] On the other hand, Hoover had, for an
even longer period, harbored the popularly held theory that unbalanced budgets, the abandonment of the gold standard, and
the use of fiat money had brought ruinous inflation to Europe.
The exigency of recovery, therefore, was an annually balanced
budget.

From the very outset of the Depression, applying the high-
wage philosophy popular in the 1920s, Hoover used his office
to persuade big business, in particular, to maintain wages. Until
early 1930 the ranks held, but by mid-1931 wage reductions
were common. These wage cuts were made not in the name of
recovery but in that of survival. The biggest blow of all came
in September 1931 when the U.S. Steel Corporation began wage
cuts of its own. For other businesses, this amounted to a signal
that the boy had taken his finger from the dike. Hoover did not
change his position, however.

By late 1931 Hoover was desperate enough to hold a series
of conferences with business and labor spokesmen. They concurred on the point, among others, that wage rates should be
maintained and that the federal and state governments should
accelerate public works programs. Only a month later, however, in his December 1931 budget message to Congress, Hoover
ruefully forewarned an anxious legislature that fiscal 1931
would see a deficit budget to the tune of $902,000,000 and that
the deficit could be as large as $2,123,000,000 in 1932. The time
had come, Hoover counseled, to reduce the deficit. Expenditures
should be so reduced and taxes so increased as to balance the
budget in fiscal 1934.

18. Committee of the President's Conference on Unemployment, *Business
Cycles and Unemployment* (New York: McGraw-Hill, 1923), p. vi.

During the same month in 1931, a subcommittee of the President's Organization on Unemployment Relief released its report. Called the Committee on the Program of Federal Public Works and stacked with contractionists such as Jacob H. Hollander and Leonard P. Ayres, this group advised that a $5 billion bond issue, such as the one proposed by W. R. Hearst and sponsored in the Senate by Robert LaFollette, would be onerous for many years. The required business readjustment simply was not a function of a public works program, inasmuch as international factors basically determined such things as the general levels of commodity prices, for example. In the long run, they argued, the private sector must solve the problems of unemployment.

By May 1932 several persuasive efforts in behalf of deficit-financed public works had been registered. In January twenty-four of America's most well-known economists (including Irving Fisher of Yale University; Alvin H. Hansen and Arthur W. Marget of the University of Minnesota; Henry Schultz, Jacob Viner, Frank H. Knight, Lloyd W. Mints, Theodore O. Yntema, Harry A. Millis, Aaron Director, and Henry C. Simons of the University of Chicago; Harold G. Moulton of Brookings; and James W. Angell of Columbia University) had telegraphed Hoover a recommendation to deficit finance a level of public works expenditures not less than fiscal 1930. Only the month before, economists' letters, overwhelmingly in support of Senator Wagner's S. 4076, had filled the *Congressional Record*. The pressure was on Hoover to answer these economists and the others who voiced similar advice.

In a 21 May 1932 reply to a query by Herbert S. Crocker (American Society of Civil Engineers), Hoover responded to the arguments of his critics. A group including Crocker had delivered to Hoover a presentation "suggesting that the depression can be broken by a large issue of Federal Government bonds to finance a new program of huge expansion of 'public works' construction, in addition to the already large programs now provided for in the current budgets."[19] Hoover admitted that this

19. Cf. William Starr Myers and Walter H. Newton, *The Hoover Administration* (New York: Charles Scribner's Sons, 1936), pp. 208–11.

same type of proposal had been made "from other quarters" and that he had given such a proposal serious consideration. Identifying the major vices which he found in these proposals for further expansion of public works, Hoover protested that "they include public works of remote usefulness; they impose unbearable burdens upon the taxpayer; they unbalance the budget and demoralize government credit." Hoover was convinced that unemployment could be relieved more effectively by increased aid to *income-producing* works. Apparently, he felt that self-liquidating public works were just as effective in dealing with unemployment, without being either burdensome to taxpayers or a danger to government credit. Most important from Hoover's point of view, the financing of income-producing public works by the Reconstruction Finance Corporation would not unbalance the budget, would not impose a drain upon the Treasury, and would not involve a direct issue of government bonds. "Non-productive public works," on the other hand, necessitated increased appropriations by the Congress, financed by increased taxation on bonds. Non-productive public works would "upset all possibility of balancing the budget," which would in turn "destroy confidence in government securities." The end was clear to Hoover. An unbalanced budget made for instability of government, which Hoover said would "deprive more people of employment than will be gained."[20]

Hoover conceded that he had been an advocate of accelerated public works in times of depression as an aid to business and unemployment. This already had been done to the limits of fiscal stability, Hoover explained. Furthermore, the new projects which might be undertaken were approaching uselessness. As evidence, Hoover pointed out that the $575,000,000 of such expenditures planned for fiscal 1933 included all the items he felt were justified by sound engineering and sound finance.

In short, then, Hoover somehow was convinced that "the balancing of the Federal budget and unimpaired national credit is indispensable to the restoration of confidence and to the very start of economic recovery." Extraordinary public works expendi-

20. Ibid.

tures were simply out of the question because they also created an enormous deficit. What was needed, Hoover argued, was a return of confidence, and this return would be impeded by attempts to issue large amounts of government bonds for purposes of nonproductive works.

In conclusion, Hoover reiterated his theory that unbalanced budgets had spawned Europe's economic troubles. He said that resorting to a so-called "extraordinary budget" would fool no one. That device, Hoover explained, had brought financial disaster to foreign governments. It meant, among other things, "an unsound financial program, and a severe blow to returning confidence and further contraction of economic activities in the country."[21]

From the very outset of the Hoover-Roosevelt campaign, Franklin D. Roosevelt tried to out-retrench his worthy opponent. If anything, Roosevelt asserted an even stronger belief in the balanced budget than Hoover had, and he sharply criticized the Hoover administration for its failure to ward off deficits. Like Hoover, he was solidly against any tampering with the gold standard. Like Hoover, Roosevelt favored large public works expenditures. And, like Hoover, he insisted that they should be self-liquidating. In short, both were convinced that the government could not squander the country into prosperity.

But Roosevelt was coalition-minded. His lot was cast with the farmer, the worker, and the debtor—with the little man. Roosevelt's plan was to raise prices by providing these favored groups with additional purchasing power. The farmers were the earmarked beneficiaries of the Farm Act (which, according to Seymour Harris, proposed to "curtail production by taxing consumers twice: once to obtain revenue to reward the farmer for curtailing production, and then by paying the higher prices that follow in the wake of curtailed production").[22] Workers were the earmarked beneficiaries of the high wage policy provided in the Recovery Act and further favored through relief

21. Ibid.
22. S. E. Harris, "The Economic Legislation of the 73rd Congress (1st session), 1933," *Economic Journal* (December 1933), p. 619.

expenditures as well as public works provided in the Recovery and Relief acts. Higher prices not only eased the burden of debts, but also resulted in workers' exploitation of other classes to the extent that prices did rise as much or as soon as wages.

This, then, was the Roosevelt strategy during the early years. Higher prices were the goal, and the higher prices were to be induced not through an active monetary or fiscal policy, which would have dispersed additional purchasing power generally, but by favoring the farmers and the workers with additional purchasing power, thus distributing gains unevenly.

The attitude of most of the economists who were cool if not hostile to Roosevelt's *omnium-gatherum* was based on the same grounds as was their objection to bonus legislation. Others, Seymour Harris for example, faulted Roosevelt for his acceptance of a rather extreme form of the high-wage theory. As Harris put it, this seemed "to predispose [Roosevelt] to coerce business enterprise to submit to an increase in labour costs beyond a point where compensation can be expected from lower non-labour costs per unit of output or may be obtained from higher prices, and raises serious doubts concerning some aspects of his programme."[23]

Roosevelt's strategy to augment selectively the incomes of farmers and workers was not without its inconsistencies. Government workers were discharged in wholesale numbers, and the lucky ones who kept their jobs had their pay reduced—all as a part of a Roosevelt economy drive necessary to help balance the budget. And this was all done at the same time that the federal government was providing relief expenditures and public works to care for the needy (many of whom were needy by virtue of having lost government jobs or having government pay reduced); requiring local governments to balance their budgets as a condition for obtaining federal public works funds; and, subsequent to their default, requiring private industry to increase its expenditures.

23. Ibid., p. 649.

Tutelaries of Retrenchment: Some Notes

While Washington opinion was by no means unanimous, the Congress and the Executive were, for the most part, unsurpassed among vocal amateur groups when it came to oratory and action in support of retrenchment. For 150 years the annually balanced budget had been equated popularly and officially with fiscal solvency and sound finance. In short, a balanced budget was esteemed as a test of fiscal management and control of government. It was hardly surprising that the reaction against unbalanced budgets was immediate and harsh. Deficit budgets were claimed to undermine a revival of confidence, to put the federal government in competition with the private sector for lendable funds (driving up the interest rate), and to guarantee inflation. At the same time, the balanced budget was regarded almost mystically as a weapon against both depression and inflation.

Some monetary economists agreed. The quantity theorists, on the other hand, argued in the strongest terms for a managed monetary and credit system geared to prices. To them, falling prices indicated an excess supply of commodities. The supply of money should be increased, therefore, until the output of a fully employed economy was cleared from the market. Whereas these quantity theorists blamed monetary authorities for contributing to the depression by not doing enough, many monetary economists contended that the depression was the result of having done too much. For example, H. Parker Willis argued from the very outset of the Depression that Treasury and Federal Reserve officials were largely responsible for the original panic. Overexpanded plants, excessive wages, and inflated prices characterized the time preceding the crash; measures to ease credit, augment wage income, and drive up prices simply failed to recognize that the Depression was caused by a capacity-wage-price maladjustment and would be ended only after a gradual readjustment had worked itself out. B. M. Anderson, Jr., monetary economist for the Chase National Bank, held practically the same views as Willis, with one notable difference. Anderson apparently approved deficit budgets during periods of depression, because a strong government with sound credit could always borrow (although it might have to pay high interest rates on loans) for short periods. If the depression were a long and severe one, however, any government presumably would be forced to cut expenses and raise taxes.

Much of the retrenchment advice was imported. For the most part, many continental European economists were committed intractably to a do-nothing government policy. At most, they reluctantly conceded to limited monetary and international adjustments. Among the most notable opinions from abroad were those of G. Cassel and J. Schumpeter. Similar to the views of Irving Fisher, Cassel favored an easy money policy and a tight budget policy. In 1930 he bitterly attacked the Hoover Administration for its accelerated public works program. Such a program could only be harmful, Cassel argued. Since there was a shortage of capital, it could not provide employment and was likely to inhibit the normal growth of capital equipment by diverting savings into the public sector. The genuine answer to the crisis, then, was for the central bank authorities to raise price levels until they agreed with the rigid wage levels. Schumpeter's views were even more in line with retrenchment. At the 1930 American Economic Association meetings, he asserted that the Depression was inevitable and that its severity was owing to wage rigidities.[24]

Consensus among Economists

During the early years of the Depression, differences over detail tended to obscure the substantial agreement on overall policy. Among economists—then as well as now—there was a measure of intraprofessional disagreement over detail. Out of concern that these controversies would mislead a public into the belief that economists were unable to agree on broad issues of

24. Schumpeter's views did change somewhat as the amplitude and the duration of the Depression became unprecedented.

public policy, and beyond that, into the approval of deleterious public policy, economists turned to the use of petitions, public statements, memoranda, and testimony in disclaiming inaction, retrenchment, and incantation as the means of recovery from depression. As evidenced by dealings with officialdom and the public-at-large, there was substantial agreement among economists regarding the use of public works. The reasoning in behalf of public works, on the other hand, was much more varied, leading to arguments for countercyclical timing of public works expenditures, to proposals for large, "one-shot," pump-priming expenditures, and to defenses of countercyclical balancing of the budget. Underlying the apparent myriad of opinions regarding detail, however, was a veritable consensus in behalf of public spending and in opposition to inaction and, still worse, perversive policy action. ▄▄

The Chicago School

IN THEIR PUBLIC ROLE, leading economists were among the leaders of a group determined to dissuade the defenders of retrenchment. In their professional role, these leading economists were concerned not so much with dissuasion as they were with persuasion. In other words, as the Depression went along, the organs of the profession itself were employed as media for resolving internal conflict over detail. Memoranda, articles, and books carried group and individual pronouncements.

Una Voce: The Chicago Foray

In a 5 May 1967 address delivered at The Law School of the University of Chicago, Professor Milton Friedman pointed out the remarkable similarities of opinion between Chicago economists and John Maynard Keynes as "to the causes of the Great Depression, the importance of monetary policy, and the need to rely extensively on fiscal policy."[1] The similarities, Friedman argued, made Chicagoans "much less susceptible to the Keynesian virus than their contemporaries in London, Eng-

---

1. Milton Friedman, "The Monetary Theory and Policy of Henry Simons," *Journal of Law and Economics*, 10 (October 1967), 7.

land, and Cambridge, Massachusetts, who were taught that the Great Depression was a necessary and ultimately healthy purgative."[2]

Friedman's argument is similar to the one made below. During the early 1930s, University of Chicago economists were involved, individually as well as collectively, in a variety of policy efforts ranging from addresses and memoranda to testimony and books. Among the most active and earliest enthusiasts confronting fellow members of the profession was Jacob Viner who lectured extensively to professional audiences throughout the States.

JACOB VINER

According to Lawrence Miller, the Chicago School of Economics crystallized during the tenures of Frank Knight, Henry Simons, and Jacob Viner, and was "consistently less enamored with Keynesian ideas and terminology than the rest of the profession."[3] There is reason to believe, however, that these three economists found Keynesian ideas in general, and Keynesian policy in particular, to be "old hat."[4]

By 1930 Jacob Viner, in particular, agreed with what Keynes was to argue sometime later: Cambridge economics was not much help in either explaining or understanding cyclical fluctuations in employment and production. In contrast to Keynes, however, Viner suggested that "the unsuitability of [the Cambridge tradition's] standard analytical procedures for analysis of 'depression' and 'boom' was the result not of general stupidity

2. Ibid., p. 9.
3. H. Lawrence Miller, Jr., "On the 'Chicago School of Economics,'" *Journal of Political Economy*, 70 (February 1962), 68.
4. There was more reason for the Chicagoans to be annoyed than enamored to hear claims that the "simple truths [that "Government should spend more and tax less in depression; and spend less and tax more in boom"] were discoveries of Keynes's which had to be repeated and repeated hundreds of times before they made the required impression" (Seymour E. Harris, *John Maynard Keynes* [New York: Charles Scribner's Sons, 1955], p. 149. Harris is probably right that many repetitions were necessary by Keynes *and* by others such as the Chicagoans.

or perverse bias on their part but of lack of professional interest in and of dedication to short-run analysis, a lack even more conspicuous in two other great schools of economic theory, the Austrian School and the Lausanne School."[5] Viner explained that, in his case, a year or so of the Great Depression convinced him of the importance of a "shift of emphasis in economic theory to short-period analysis" and, as the degree of the crisis grew greater, of the importance of "the forces whose impact was predominately short-run in character."[6]

Viner's recollections of his early Depression professional persuasion are clearly borne out by the evidence. In 1931 the Eleventh Session of the Institute of Politics at Williamstown, Massachusetts, invited Viner to lead round tables on "Problems of International Commercial and Financial Policy."[7] At the seventh meeting of his round table, Viner discussed and criticized prevailing American Treasury policy. The Treasury, he explained, was still practicing traditional policies based on so-called sound principles of finance: taxing heavily, spending lightly, and redeeming debts. Admitting that such practices might be sound policies during periods of prosperity and expansion, Viner argued that they were unwise and inappropriate depression policies. "When business activity is declining, or is stagnant and at a low level," Viner contended, "reduced taxation, and budget deficits are, from the point of view of the national economy as a whole, sound policy rather than unsound."[8]

It would appear that Viner (dubbed "the Twentieth Century Ricardian" by Dorfman) also discovered the "simple truths" of modern fiscal policy. "This formula [that government should spend more and tax less in depression and spend less and tax more in boom] may have been a discovery of Keynes," Viner asserted, "but I used it at least as early as the summer of 1931, and I don't think I derived it from Keynes, with whose jour-

5. Jacob Viner, "Comment on 1936 Review," p. 254.
6. Ibid., pp. 255–56.
7. Arthur Howland Buffington (ed.), *Report of the Round Tables and General Conferences at the Eleventh Session* (Williamstown, Mass.: The Institute of Politics, 1931).
8. Ibid., p. 182.

nalistic writings I then had little acquaintance."[9] Disclaiming the role of discoverer or pioneer, Viner further argued that "the idea was then commonplace in my academic surroundings of the time, and I cannot recall that any of my Chicago colleagues would have dissented, or that they needed to learn it from Keynes, or from me."[10]

At the Williamstown meetings Viner explained that, of an estimated seventy billion dollars of annual expenditure in the United States, twenty-five to thirty billion dollars was by either governmental or quasi-public agencies. Such expenditures were practically exogenous, Viner argued, going on regardless of business conditions and not subject to depression psychology. The other forty to forty-five billion dollars was affected by depression conditions in such a way that capital became idle and laborers became unemployed involuntarily. This need not be, Viner suggested. During depression, government could borrow to defray expenditures which would give rise to the employment of otherwise idle capital and labor. Furthermore, he continued, "in so far as the funds spent by the Government are primarily financed by tax money which otherwise would be hoarded and saved, or by borrowing from existent funds which otherwise would remain uninvested, or by expansion of bank credit which otherwise would remain unexploited, the public works or other useful government services so financed during a period of economic depression are from the national economic point of view almost costless. . . ."[11]

As the Depression deepened, Viner continued to lecture widely on policy alternatives. In 1933 he delivered two papers in which he most explicitly considered policy trends. In *Balanced Deflation, Inflation, or More Depression,* a paper delivered in the Day and Hour Series of the University of Minnesota, Viner granted that the individual could do nothing either to end or to escape depressions once they were under way. He then treated the more important question of whether there

9. Viner, "Comment on 1936 Review," p. 264.
10. Ibid.
11. Buffington, *Report of the Round Tables,* p. 183.

was likewise nothing which individuals could do collectively to either abate the depression's severity or restore prosperity. Accordingly, Viner considered five policies: (1) the "do-nothing" or "let nature take its course" or "painful waiting" policy; (2) the hortatory or incantation policy; (3) the "do the wrong things" policy; (4) the induced balanced deflation policy; and (5) the inflation policy.[12] The policies implied in the title of Viner's paper are the only ones which are really noteworthy.

First of all, Viner admitted that if the economy mirrored the assumptions which characterized it as perfectly flexible and immediately responsive to change, the "do-nothing" argument might have much strength. "In a perfectly flexible economy where money costs and prices quickly adjust themselves to changed circumstances," he stated, "there could be price level fluctuations, or fluctuations in the real income of labor, but there could not be substantial fluctuations of employment or production."[13] Viner noted that whereas the "do-nothing" view of our economic system implicitly rested on the assumption of price flexibility, in fact, the price structure was shot through with rigidities. In view of these real world rigidities, Viner called the advocates of the "do-nothing" policy the advocates of inertia and of painful waiting. Convinced that there was an ominous possibility of wholesale economic collapse, Viner bitterly charged that we already had been waiting at least three years too long.

Viner considered the argument for "induced balanced deflation" little more than a mistaken supposition. If costs were reduced as rapidly as and to the extent of prices, it was supposed that pre-depression price and cost relationships could be restored. A year before, however, Viner had joined his colleagues in arguing that deflation of costs was impracticable politically and would be voided in some cases by unemployment, anyway.[14] Actually, in the 1933 case Viner seriously discussed induced balanced defla-

12. Jacob Viner, *Balanced Deflation, Inflation, or More Depression* (Minneapolis, Minn.: University of Minnesota Press, no. 3, The Day and Hour Series of the University of Minnesota, April 1933), p. 6.
13. Ibid., p. 9.
14. Committee on Ways and Means, *Hearings*, p. 524.

tion only because he felt that it was professionally necessary to consider policies within the real world context of a gold standard. That is, given the gold standard as an institution around which economic policy had to be molded, cost reduction was a safe method by which a gold country could attempt unilaterally to induce economic recovery.

At this point Viner carefully and somewhat bitterly criticized the "fear campaign" directed toward deficit budgets. It had excited groundless anxieties which unnecessarily jeopardized a sound policy. In other words, Viner was arguing again just as he and his Chicago colleagues had argued since the outset of the Depression, that countercyclical balancing of the budget was sound fiscal practice but that a fear campaign, alleging the adverse effects of deficits, had rendered this otherwise sound policy hazardous. "For the federal government," Viner complained, "the campaign for balancing the budget has made it dangerous to increase the debt substantially because of the adverse effect it would have on the morale of a sacred public taught to measure the stability of government by a financial record for a single year or short period of years."[15]

Viner made it clear that, in the absence of ill-advised fears, countercyclical deficit financing was sound fiscal policy during depressions. "Had it not been for this campaign fear," Viner argued, "it would have been sound policy on the part of the federal government deliberately to permit a deficit to accumulate during depression years, to be liquidated during prosperity years from the higher productivity of the tax system and from increases in tax rates when they would do no harm."[16] By his oft repeated fears of deficit financing, however, Hoover had undermined the constructive effects even of his involuntary deficits. In Viner's words, "The outstanding though unintentional achievement of the Hoover Administration in counteracting the depression has in fact been its deficits of the last two years, and it was only its own alleged fears as to the ill effects of these deficits, and the panic which the business world pro-

15. Viner, *Balanced Deflation,* p. 18.
16. Ibid., pp. 18–19.

fessed to foresee if these deficits should recur, which have made this method of depression finance seriously risky."[17] In a spirit of downright commiseration, Viner concluded that "had the government and the business magnates retained their mental balance, there would have been less cause to fear net ill effects during a depression than during the war from even a ten billion dollar deficit."[18]

Viner's discussion of inflation as a policy was elaborated into a major paper delivered only a few months later in 1933.[19] It was in Georgia that Viner felt most free to strongly advance inflation, especially fiscal inflation. He pointed out that once a country was off gold, as was the United States by May 1933, the balanced-deflation argument was deprived even of its weak justification.

Viner explained the efficacy of inflation in general, as a depression remedy. "The process of putting purchasing power into circulation will operate to increase the total volume of money income," he proclaimed.[20] The mechanism which Viner had in mind was one whereby prices would tend to rise (but proportionately less than business expenditures) and physical output would consequently increase, meaning an increased employment of productive factors. Viner also pointed out that prices would rise more than costs, causing a fall in real wages (W/P) without any downward pressure on money wages (W). Here, he admitted, one might be hard put to demonstrate theoretically that prices would rise faster than costs, but inflations in reality worked out that way. Wages and other costs simply lagged behind prices, providing an important stimulus to increased employment and production during an upward trend of prices.

In terms of particulars, Viner recommended that the most promising method of combating a depression was "that of governmental expenditures financed by borrowing from the banking

17. Ibid.
18. Ibid.
19. Jacob Viner, "Inflation as a Remedy for Depression," *Proceedings of the Institute of Public Affairs, Seventh Annual Session* (Athens, Ga.: University of Georgia, 1933).
20. Ibid., p. 122.

system, with the hope that what the banks lend is newly created credit or credit which otherwise would have remained idle. . . ."[21] Viner made it clear that sound principles of public finance justified unbalanced budgets. During depression, government clearly should incur an excess of expenditures over revenues, the deficit being financed by either creating new bank credit or resorting to the printing press. By this time (1933) Viner was impatient with his antagonists and lashed out bitterly at them, charging that "there is nothing as unsound as hoary doctrines that have acquired the support of authority simply because they are traditional and have stood for so long without genuinely critical examination. One of these mouldy fallacies is that regardless of circumstances the government must balance its budget in each year. Why not in each month or week or hour?"[22]

Then, Viner advanced a notion which, by 1933, the Chicago economists largely had helped to make familiar. If the budget was to be balanced, it should be balanced over the business cycle as the outcome of using public spending to compensate for changes in private spending. Viner thus affirmed once again the "simple truths" of compensatory public finance, i.e., governments should accumulate deficits during depressions and surpluses during boom periods, either building up cash reserves or liquidating outstanding debt as conditions indicate.

Within the profession Jacob Viner was an economist of no little influence by the early 1930s. His reputation in international economics long since had been made and his contributions to value theory, especially to the theory of perfect competition, were recognized widely during this period. Well known as a theoretician, Viner was, moreover, concerned with economic policy. Along with his colleagues at the University of Chicago, he launched more than one attack on the sponsors of retrenchment. Viner recognized that at less than full employment outputs, expansionary fiscal policy should be administered to induce movements toward increased output and employment of productive factors. The whole notion of balancing the budget over the

21. Ibid., p. 133.
22. Ibid., p. 129.

business cycle, for that matter, was linked directly to the notion of full employment output. But it was really through the pen of Paul H. Douglas (1934), writing under the influence of J. M. Clark, that these two notions were wedded most carefully by a Chicagoan.

PUBLIC POLICY PAMPHLET NO. 1

Meanwhile, Viner was also working with many of his Chicago colleagues to publish *Balancing the Budget*.[23] In the very first paragraph of their statement, they (notably, Paul H. Douglas, Simeon E. Leland, H. A. Millis, Henry C. Simons, and Jacob Viner) warned readers of the retarding effects which annually balanced budgets have during depressions. "There appears to be grave danger that in balancing its budget the federal government may adopt policies," they disclosed, "the inevitable consequence of which will be the retardation of business recovery and the impairment of the social usefulness of government."[24]

In rebuttal to prevailing Treasury and Executive philosophy, the Chicagoans argued that it was not axiomatic that the federal government should collect annual revenues sufficient to defray even its ordinary operating expenses. Indeed, they listed several types of expenditures which should not be financed by taxation, but rather with short-term borrowing, long-term funding, or issuance of fiat money: (1) nonrecurrent emergency expenditures, (2) loans and investments, (3) expenditures for public works, (4) permanent appropriations not to be spent during the current fiscal year, and (5) public debt retirements.

Then, the Chicago group reiterated the argument which

23. Frank Bane et al., *Balancing the Budget* (Chicago: University of Chicago Press, 1933; Public Policy Pamphlet No. 1). Reprinted in *Contemporary Problems in the United States*, ed. Horace Taylor (New York: Harcourt, Brace and Co., 1934–35). The statement was signed by Frank Bane, Paul Betters, Carl Chatters, Paul H. Douglas, Simeon E. Leland, H. A. Millis, Clarence E. Ridley, H. C. Simons, Donald Slesinger, Jacob Viner, and L. D. White.
24. Ibid., p. 1.

it had made before every conceivable type of audience: "The balancing of budgets should be regarded as a series of long-term operations in which deficits will be incurred and debts increased during years of economic adversity while Treasury surpluses and the rapid retirement of the public debt will be planned for during years of prosperity."[25] They continued with a familiar theme: "When a series of annual budgets is thus put together, the result is the balancing of the long-term budget with reference to economic cycle periods. The equilibrium between revenue and expenditures is thus intentionally struck over a period of years rather than annually."[26]

The Chicagoans were convinced openly that if annually balanced budgets were maintained during depressions, the result would prolong the depression. In other words, the repercussions of fiscal policy on the nation's currency system clearly could not be ignored. During economic adversity the flow of funds in industry and commerce was favorably affected by borrowing to support the volume of public expenditures, they argued. Taxation as the means of supporting these expenditures, on the other hand, would detract from the very credit created by the expenditures. It was obvious to the Chicago group, therefore, that government should finance emergency expenditures, investments, and public works by borrowing instead of taxation.

PAUL H. DOUGLAS

In 1934 Professor Paul H. Douglas pieced together much of what he and his colleagues had been doing since the early 1930s and combined it with the work of Wicksell, Keynes, Clark, and others. The result was a book, *Controlling Depressions*, published in 1935.[27] In the Preface Douglas disclosed the nature of the problems he had treated and the origin of his concern with

---

25. Ibid., p. 4.
26. Ibid., p. 10.
27. Paul H. Douglas, *Controlling Depressions* (New York: W. W. Norton & Co., 1935).

them. "[T]he stirring flow of events during periods of upheaval and social change," he stated, "compel [economists] to turn their attention to the problems of practical adjustment."[28] In addressing himself to these problems, Douglas assigned himself the tasks of analyzing the main causes of the Depression and of pointing out ways in which future depressions might be reduced, if not eliminated.

Douglas saw in depressions both "initiating" and "cumulative" causes. Whatever the initiating cause which throws business out of equilibrium, the slightest depression "may continually get worse, and production, employment and purchasing power may be cumulatively destroyed," Douglas argued.[29] And depression manifested itself in the causal order implied by that statement; namely, there is first a decrease in production, causing a decrease in employment, causing a decrease in purchases and in purchasing power.

Douglas moreover pointed out that, in any depression, the decrease in the production of capital goods is greater than that in the production of consumer goods. "This can be stated in more precise mathematical terms," Douglas asserted, "by saying that the demand for capital goods is a function not only of the total demand for consumer goods but rather of the rate of change in the demand for these latter products."[30] Economists will recognize this as an early statement of the *acceleration principle*. In Douglas's case, his early understanding of this principle is probably owing to his association with J. M. Clark.

Douglas joined E. R. Walker,[31] Keynes, and others in pointing out the weaknesses of an older tradition in economics which assumed that savings were identically equal to investment. "Purchasing power was, therefore, treated, like the grace of God, as transferable but indestructible," Douglas charged.[32] Drawing on the work of Knut Wicksell and J. M. Keynes's *Treatise*, Douglas pointed to the saving-investment nexus as the major

28. Ibid., p. v.
29. Ibid., p. 10.
30. Ibid., p. 13.
31. Cf. E. Ronald Walker, *Unemployment Policy* (Sydney, Australia: Angus & Robertson Ltd., 1936).
32. Douglas, *Controlling Depressions*, p. 29.

culprit in depression making. The sperm of a depression was an excess of saving over investment. During such a period, deposits flowed into banks through savings but they did not flow out to any appreciable degree through investments. The result, Douglas argued, was a reduced flow of purchasing power or spending. Unemployment and decreased business hit the consumer goods industries with no corresponding or neutralizing increase in the producer goods industries—indeed, there was an even greater decrease in business, hence employment, in the latter industries. As production and prices fell, wage rates became difficult to maintain. If money wages were maintained so that real wages increased beyond marginal productivity, unemployment was further increased. If wages were reduced along with prices, there was a likelihood of a diminishing flow of purchasing power.

Douglas differed with Wicksell and Keynes insofar as he saw in the saving-investment nexus a "cumulative," not an "initiating," cause of depression. That is, Douglas thought that Wicksell and Keynes deserved credit for pointing out that there is no necessary identity between savings and investments. However, he felt that they were describing characteristics of booms and depressions and were not explaining what gave rise to prosperity or depression in the first place. For example, during prosperity, investments exceeded savings because capital could earn a higher rate of interest than that charged in the market. But why, Douglas queried, were earnings of capital so high? In the depression case, savings exceeded investments because capital could not earn a rate of interest high enough to pay that which was charged in the market. Again, Douglas queried, why would earnings on capital be so low? Douglas traced the fundamental causes of depression to industry's failure either to reduce prices or to increase wages in the face of a rapidly increasing output. In short, there simply was not enough spending to sustain a rate of output which was spurred by the large profits and undue investment which resulted from this failure.

Paul Douglas clearly pointed to changes in the *rate* of investment as the initiating cause of depression. Unlike Keynes, Douglas largely concentrated on endogenous changes in investment, which arose principally from wage-price considerations. Douglas did not ignore exogenous changes, however. Several times in his discussion, he pointed out the effects of changes in expectations on investment.

Douglas was critical of the J. B. Say tradition which reasoned that the production of goods generated the demand for goods and that consequently no overproduction could exist. The Say tradition, Douglas argued, ignored both the possibility of producing more goods than could be consumed at a given price level and the harmful effects *(ex post* and *ex ante)* on business which sharply reduced prices would have. Since modern production involved the prior payment of money costs for resources and bank credit which the business then attempted to recoup out of the selling price, expectations of returns played an important role in investment. When the future appeared to hold prospects for lower returns, then modern business would be expected to respond with curtailed investment, curtailed production, curtailed purchases of raw materials, and curtailed employment of labor.

Would a depression inevitably cure itself? The true believers that it would, Douglas said, rested their case on any or all three of the following grounds: (1) an appeal to the historical fact that recovery followed every previous depression; (2) a fundamental belief in the economic vitality of the capitalistic system; and (3) the assumed tendencies of a depression to generate naturally the economic conditions to develop renewed prosperity. Douglas dismissed the first two arguments easily enough, but he took more care in undermining the third.

Not unlike the way in which Pigou was attacked by Keynes, Wesley Mitchell was the subject of a Douglas onslaught.[33] In his *Business Cycles* (1913), Mitchell had argued that three sets of economic forces inevitably bred revival: (1) an increase in consumer demands; (2) an increase in investment of savings; and (3) a decrease in costs caused by internal, structural changes. The mechanism which Mitchell had in mind begins with the general

33. Cf. Wesley C. Mitchell, *Business Cycles* (Berkeley: University of California Press, 1913).

exhaustion, after a time, of consumer inventories. As stocks are replenished, the demand for consumer goods increases. Added to this increased flow of consumer spending is an increased flow of replacement investment spending. The second part of Mitchell's mechanism is a sharp increase, after a time, in investment of new capital. Since savings have been accumulating in banks and interest rates are low, businessmen are strongly encouraged to borrow these sums and construct new capacity to produce the increased output now demanded by consumers. Finally, the depression can also be expected to increase the output per man hour (least efficient workers are unemployed) and hence decrease the labor costs per unit, consequently restoring a satisfactory profit margin.

Douglas admitted that Mitchell's argument had appeal, but at the same time he clearly recognized its fundamental illogic. In the first place, Mitchell obviously was assuming that consumers would have the money income to replenish their inventories. The point was, however, that a depression greatly reduced the purchasing power of workers and consumers, and likewise reduced the possibility of their acquiring the money to increase their purchases in the way Mitchell assumed. Douglas also denied that savings accumulate during a depression. In brief, Douglas demonstrated that the policy of doing nothing towards counteracting business depressions was a mistake destined to bring about a chronic equilibrium or disequilibrium of unemployment of resources and bad times in general. "Without vigorous constructive action," Douglas concluded, "even ultimate recovery is by no means certain, while it is, in any event, likely to be long-delayed."[34]

Douglas now was prepared to consider the question of vigorous constructive action. He first considered monetary policy. Particularly during the mid-twenties, a large group of economists had suggested that the Federal Reserve system had sufficient powers to stabilize the price level and prevent depressions. Price stability was thought to be simply a matter of manipulating the

34. Douglas, *Controlling Depressions*, p. 95.

rediscount rate on commercial paper and using open-market operations. Both tools worked on the interest rate, helping to make the market rate of interest equal the "natural" rate (in the Wicksell and Keynes tradition).

Paul Douglas was not convinced that the manipulation of rediscount rates and open-market operations would affect booms more than slightly, and he asserted that they were still less effective in dealing with depression. In the first place, lowering the rediscount rate at a time when banks were accumulating idle reserves, which suggested they had no particular reason or need to resort to rediscounting in order to make loans would not likely stimulate borrowing. In any case, it was not short-term interest rates which inhibited borrowing. What inhibited borrowing in a period of contraction was the fear that borrowing additional sums to expand output would result in goods left on hand because of a lack of purchases.[35]

As for the open-market operations, there was every reason why this attempt should have collapsed, as it did during 1929–33. The notion was that the payments for bonds would build up the flow of bank reserves, which banks would lend to industry rather than leave idle. This money then would be used by industry to expand current output of consumer goods, replace and add to capital equipment, and augment the employment of labor. Both consumer and investor spending was expected to increase, therefore. Douglas pointed out this policy had been used as early as October 1929 ($300 million of securities bought in two months), but it had little or no permanent effect upon the depression, which increased in severity month by month. Douglas was certain that $1 billion would not have helped at all.

To Douglas, the reason for failure was clear. Depression did

---

35. In Douglas's words, "Business does not want to borrow for long-time purposes, since with a large portion of its present factories and machines idle, it certainly does not desire to add to them. On the contrary, its policy is to utilize its existing plant far more fully before it begins to construct more. [Therefore, the acceleration principle is unimportant until demand threatens to exceed existing capacity.] Nor is any one business desirous of borrowing much more on short-time loans in order to expand the current output of consumers goods, since it does not know that there will be sufficient added purchasing power in the hands of consumers to take the added quantity of the particular commodity off the market as a profit" (ibid., p. 118).

not demand extending cash loans to banks; what it called for as a remedy were bank loans to businesses at a time when businesses feared to borrow and banks feared to lend. The failure of monetary policy, therefore, could be traced to expectations.

The rediscount rate and open-market operations, Douglas argued, were both "weak reeds." If they could not be counted on to stabilize the economy at a high rate of employment, then what could? Douglas's answer, like that of his Chicago colleagues, was "public works and fiscal policy."

Under the heading of "The Commonsense of Public Works," Douglas asserted that the justification for a large added volume of public works during a depression was simple. First, it used resources which otherwise would be idle. Making the point that Viner and others had made much earlier, Douglas pointed out that "in a sense, the works carried through are socially costless, since if they were not built nothing else would have been done with the labor."[36] Second, the total production of goods was stimulated by considerably more than the amounts directly spent. The laborers and owners of raw materials would have incomes which they otherwise would not have had and spend money which they otherwise would not have spent, consequently augmenting the incomes and spending of others. There was leakage in this process, inasmuch as some of the added purchasing power would not create an additional demand for domestic goods. Some would replace relief expenditures, and some would be offset by potential increases in prices. Some would be hoarded, and some spent on foreign goods. Following the leads of Kahn and Keynes, however, Douglas guessed that most of each dollar would not be so absorbed but would instead constitute an increased effective demand for commodities and services.[37]

After allowing for relief payments, hoarding ("slight in view of the urgent needs of the population"), purchases of foreign

36. Ibid., p. 123.
37. Ibid., pp. 123–24. Cf. J. M. Keynes, *The Means to Prosperity* (New York: Harcourt, Brace and Co., 1933); R. F. Kahn, "The Relation of Home Investment to Unemployment," *Economic Journal,* 41 (June 1931), 173–98; R. F. Kahn, "Public Works and Inflation," *Journal of the American Statistical Association,* 27 (March 1933 Supplement), 168–73.

goods (could be "an indirect stimulus to production"), and probable price increases, Douglas estimated that sixty-five per cent of each dollar would be passed on as increased real purchasing power. Since Douglas viewed the multiplier as an approximation, he did not reduce it to formulation. Instead, he was satisfied to measure roughly the total relative effect of each dollar spent for public works by applying a constant ratio to a series of diminishing magnitudes. The indirect or secondary effect of a dollar's expenditure by government, assuming that leakage amounted to 35 per cent, was approximately $1.80, Douglas said. The total effect, therefore, was somewhere around $2.80.[38]

Points such as these, Douglas asserted, many "so-called 'orthodox' critics" of public works expenditures completely missed. These critics were plainly mistaken in assuming (1) full employment of workers and plants, and (2) a constant supply of goods. These critics thereby reached the mistaken conclusion that the creation of additional monetary purchasing power would result simply in a proportionate increase in the price level which, in turn, would reduce the effective purchasing power of others to the same extent that it built up the purchasing power of those on public works. In fact, however, the creation of purchasing power would succeed in drawing into a productive working relationship the enormous supply of unemployed labor and the correspondingly huge amount of unutilized capital which existed. The volume of production would increase because of and simultaneously with the increase in this purchasing power, and it would grow to a magnitude far beyond that provided for by the initial government expenditure.

Douglas was altogether unsympathetic toward those who believed that a government's road to ruin was paved with public works. These were the critics who argued that shrunken incomes could not withstand additional taxation, and that the alternative—deficit budgets—would bring a nation to bankruptcy. Erroneously reasoning from an analogy with the individual, this school saw the only safe policy to be that of balancing the govern-

---

38. In Keynes's formulation, $\frac{1}{m.p.s.}$, the total effect is approximately $2.85714, or exactly 2 6/7 dollars.

ment budget at all times, in periods of both depression and prosperity. Insofar as such a perverse notion called for curtailment of government expenditures during a depression, Douglas countered, the number of unemployed would increase and the quantity of purchasing power would decrease, making matters worse rather than better. To advocate balancing the budget in a period of depression, he concluded, was to campaign for the intensification of unemployment.

Having been a part of the Chicago foray for compensatory public finance from the very beginning, Douglas could not pass up this opportunity to expound their mutually embraced notion of balancing the budget over the business cycle. "[W]hile the government budget should normally balance over the period of a major cycle as a whole," Douglas proclaimed as proxy for the Chicago group as a whole, "it need not and indeed should not do so in each and every year."[39] The "simple truths" of compensatory public finance were well known to Douglas just as they were to his Chicago colleagues. According to Douglas's version:

[D]uring depressions the government should increase its expenditure not only for relief but also for public works. In so doing it will help to offset the decline in private business. Then as prosperity returns the government receipts will rise and public expenditures for relief and works will be rapidly tapered off. A surplus will now replace the former deficit and this should be devoted to paying off the bonds sold or non-interest bearing treasury notes which may have been issued during the depression. Government expenditures should in short, move against the current of private business, expanding as the latter contracts and contracting as the latter expands.[40]

Douglas then explained that an expanded public works (and relief) program, in general, could be financed from three sources —taxes, bonds, and treasury notes (paper money). The first of these, taxation, was an ineffective means to promote recovery, inasmuch as it resulted merely in a transfer of purchasing power rather than in an increase of it. The only exception to this gen-

39. Douglas, *Controlling Depressions*, p. 125.
40. Ibid.

eralization was the case where revenue derived from taxing income hoarded by individuals or banks was used to provide employment for idle labor, and then was spent by those who received it as payment for their services. In this process, aggregate
spending, employment, and production were all stimulated.
"Since it is the well-to-do who have the largest hoards," Douglas
commented, "it follows that while taxation as a whole is inferior
during a depression to the other two methods of financing,
highly progressive income taxes are the least, and sales taxes
the most objectionable forms of taxation which could be used."[41]
To Paul Douglas, the unfortunate fact that so many governments
had turned to sales taxation during the Great Depression was a
cause for sadness as well as criticism.

The other two methods of financing an expanded public
works program—borrowing and monetary issue—clearly added
to purchasing power, and hence, to employment and production.
Once more, Douglas explicitly identified the mistakes of those
who opposed using such methods during a depression. Some of
the critics, he stated, mistakenly assumed that public borrowing
merely drew loans away from the private sector without increasing total production. Others instead held the mistaken notion
that increases in bank credit or the money supply merely resulted in multiplying the number of monetary counters offered
for a constant supply of goods and, therefore, in a proportionate
increase in the general price level.

At the root of this opposition to governmental borrowing
and monetary issue in a depression, Douglas again saw his already cited nemesis, the assumption that all workers and all
capital are employed at such times so that production cannot be
increased, and its equally mistaken corollary, the assumption
that purchasing power can only be transferred but never destroyed or increased. The truth was, Douglas countered, the very

41. Ibid., p. 137. This is similar in some ways to the notion of the balanced
budget multiplier. Douglas is arguing that a balanced budget increase in
government activity might increase spending, employment, and production
because of differences in propensities to spend. He even goes so far as to
recognize that the impact is greater as the differences in propensities to spend
increase.

essence of a depression consisted in massive unemployment of laborers alongside a massive volume of idle capital. Augmenting purchasing power put these otherwise idle resources into production. But what were the relative merits of loans as opposed to monetary issue in financing an expanded public works program?

If the question of money versus bonds was examined dispassionately, Douglas alleged, the issuance of money to finance public works would be judged preferable to borrowing because it was more expansionary. Although banks would use otherwise idle credit resources to subscribe for bonds, and individuals otherwise hoarded balances, Douglas thought it probable that some persons would decrease private investments in order to subscribe to the public bond issue. To the extent to which the latter was done, there would be a transfer and not a creation of purchasing power. On the other hand, a monetary issue would represent a completely fresh creation of and a net addition to total purchasing power. The only major threat to the stimulative effect of a monetary issue was the possibility of a frightened banking community unwilling to make loans.

The public works program which was being proposed, primarily would increase employment and production, Douglas declared, but, he added, an increase in total purchasing power might raise prices to some degree as well. The latter possibility troubled him. Under an international gold standard, a rising price level within the United States and the failure of other countries to adopt policies which would raise their price levels correspondingly, surely would result in an unfavorable balance of payments for the United States, which would be settled by shipping gold abroad and thus reducing national reserves. Douglas's verdict was that it would be virtually impossible for any one nation by itself to stem the tide of a worldwide depression as long as it insisted upon clinging to the gold standard.

This consideration led Douglas to conclude that President Roosevelt's monetary policy was far more creditable than his critics admitted. That is, it had been wise after all to abandon gold *before* embarking on a program which augmented employment by expanding public works and, in turn, raised the prices of farm output. Otherwise, the United States might have been driven off gold *after* this policy had been started, and, in the meanwhile, it would have been largely drained of gold. More important, if the nation had clung to the gold standard, the drain on gold might have tempted the government to abandon the policies of reemployment and reflation. In opting for a public works program rather than gold, Roosevelt had taken the right course, Douglas thought.

One issue which Douglas had avoided so far was the question of an indicator. What indicator should policy makers and advisors regard as a signal of depression? Douglas maintained that government authorities should heed the index of unemployment. As long as unemployment amounted to no more than four or five per cent (or was caused by seasonal fluctuations) there was little probability that additional credit for the financing of public works would be needed. Correspondingly, Douglas considered an unemployment index which rose to eight or ten per cent, a clear sign of impending depression. Observing this signal, the Federal Reserve system, he declared, should create credit to loan to the federal government for the financing of public works, and thereby provide the purchasing power needed to put idle labor back to work.

A vital test comes, Douglas indicated, when the public works program tapers off, if not ceases. Would the economic system then absorb workers who had been employed on public projects? Douglas considered the multiple stimulus provided to private business by the public works expenditures a major factor in making this possible. Although he counted on the multiplier principle to aid in private absorption of these laborers, Douglas was a bit uneasy about the prospects for recovery of the economic system. If too small a scale of public works were undertaken and if business failed to respond sufficiently, there would be nothing to do except to increase the loans for public works. With this point, Douglas made it very clear that if the present economic order when aided by loans for public works could not keep unemployment down to approximately eight or ten per cent, then it could not expect to continue without further modification.

In the case of Paul Douglas we have witnessed an American

economist who built an explanation of and a remedy for depression largely along Keynesian lines. He cited at every opportunity the tradition of economic thought (viz., Wicksell, Robertson, and the pre-1936 Keynes) which led him to his conclusions. Like Keynes, he did disavow an older tradition of aggregate economics, principally identified with J. B. Say, whose followers treated total effective demand as transferable, but incapable of creation or destruction.

Douglas was not as concerned with the initiating causes of depression as he was with the cumulative causes. Drawing on Wicksell and Keynes, he pointed to the disparity of saving and investment as the major cumulative cause of depression and to changes in the rate of investment as the major initiating cause of depression. The latter was aggravated by the accelerator principle in the downswing.

When he used the term "purchasing power," Douglas always meant total effective demand or total spending, a usage he made clear when he discussed Mitchell's business cycle theory. Douglas did not really make use of an aggregate supply function, although he did discuss briefly his production function in accounting for increases in production. In common with many of his American contemporaries, Douglas simply argued that if the aggregate output necessary to fully employ resources exceeded aggregate demand (i.e., total spending), there would be unemployment. The remedy was to increase total spending to the point where aggregate supply at full employment would be cleared from the market.

If manipulation of aggregate spending was the key to clearing the market of full employment output, then balancing of the budget was a flagrant abuse of policy. To Douglas, the correct remedy contradicted the traditional belief in a balanced budget. If total spending (private and nonpolicy public spending) fell short of full employment output, then public spending should be increased to sufficiently augment spending so as to clear the market of such an output. This recovery spending should be financed by bonds or newly printed money if private spending was to be maintained.

Douglas's treatise cannot really be dismissed as an *ad hoc* or an *ad hominem* piece of professional literature. He had an explanation of economic aberrations and a remedy for them. Moreover, he represented in the views he articulated a group of remarkable economists, whose unanimity of purpose and of response to economic depression was exceeded perhaps only by its outspokenness.

MEMORANDUM ON PUBLIC CREDIT

An unsigned document widely circulated within the profession and among policymakers, the *Memorandum on Public Credit* discloses several interesting features of the Chicagoans' thought.[42] It too reiterates the oft-mentioned proposal for balancing the budget over the busines cycle, but beyond that, it expresses other dimensions of their thought and reveals a modified disagreement within their ranks.

The overriding concern of the *Memorandum* was the problem of the pro-cyclical activities of state and local governments, which largely had stalemated the federal government's attempt to augment purchasing power and credit. Setting forth a method of dealing with this problem, the *Memorandum* advanced the notion that all levels of government should engage in long-range fiscal planning, i.e., balance their respective budgets over significantly long periods of time rather than annually.

The *Memorandum* deplored the reduction in purchasing power, severances from service, and nonpayment of wages inflicted upon vast numbers of public employees. In unusual and ambiguous terminology, the *Memorandum* argued that this reduction in the purchasing power of public employees rested on the assumption that a greater "social return" could be derived from such reductions than from transferring funds from "other people" to the "public employees." On the contrary, it contended, if the funds are collected, either by loans or taxes, from "other people" who have "a surplus above current needs" and who are "above the level of those to whom payments are to be

42. *Memorandum on Public Credit* (mimeographed, and circulated in various drafts during 1934–36).

made," the transfer will then "enhance social welfare." "Under a progressive tax system" the *Memorandum* continued, "the greater the degree of progression above the economic minimum the greater will be the social enhancements." If the system is regressive, however, "welfare will be minimized."[43]

The authors' confidence in tax methods which decrease the propensities to save and increase the propensities to spend was most clearly stated in the following: "To the extent that the tax policy produces a more equitable distribution of wealth and/or income, or retards the rate of capital accumulation where property ownership is already badly skewed, tendencies helpful to recovery may be anticipated."[44] The tacit assumption here is that saving and spending are functions of the relation between income and/or wealth and current needs. Despite the unusual terminology in which they had cast their argument, the point they advanced was hardly uncommon. They had advocated a policy, in this case a tax policy, to enhance total spending which they considered the factor essential to social recovery.

Perhaps the most interesting aspect of this *Memorandum* is Henry C. Simons's *private* objection to part of it. Simons had not failed to endorse a single document jointly published by the Chicago economists. Throughout the Chicago foray for compensatory public spending and countercyclical balancing of the budget, in other words, Simons played an active role. In his privately written commentary on the early draft of the *Memorandum,* Simons declared that "all this talk about long-term budget planning or budget balancing is piffle." In Henry Simons's opinion, the "immediate fiscal problem" was "that of coping with and escaping from the depression." Arguments, Simons continued, "should be stated merely in terms of what should be done now." In short, "There is no sense in fiscal planning for a cycle which no one can forecast; the problem is always one of judgment in an immediate situation."[45]

43. Ibid., p. 8.
44. Ibid.
45. Henry Simons's typed commentary on the *Memorandum.* Cf. J. Ronnie Davis, "Henry Simons, the Radical: Some Documentary Evidence," *History of Political Economy,* 1 (Fall 1969), 388–94.

Henry Simons apparently signed all of the Chicago documents out of the conviction that a unified effort in behalf of immediate deficit financing was more important than the general rationale behind this policy. Simons was further convinced that it was expenditures which were inflationary and taxation which was counter-inflationary. During depression, public expenditures should be increased, without taxation to defray them, and continued until the economy fully recovered. During booms, taxation should be increased, without any change in expenditure, and continued until the economy fully recovered. Other than these considerations, Simons had none. He did not sympathize privately with the view that these expenditure-taxation manipulations should be part of a fiscal rule to balance the budget over the business cycle.

Chicago and Stabilization Policy

In Milton Friedman's view, to reiterate, the ideas which were in the air at the University of Chicago and in the early- and mid-thirties made Chicagoans much less susceptible to the Keynesian virus than students in London and Cambridge. The evidence appears to bear out this point. Individually and collectively, before myriad audiences, the Chicagoans stressed the need to rely extensively on fiscal policy during depressions. From the very outset of the 1930s, they championed—even repeated hundreds of times in order to make the required impression—the simple truths of compensatory public finance. Their points were usually, but not always, made less out of a concern for recovery than out of an interest in stabilization. In isolation, the former would have smacked of *ad hoc* remedies. Throughout the Chicagoans' contributions, there is the notion that total spending, private plus public, should be great enough to take off the markets an output associated with full employment and stable prices. The argument constituted a type of macroeconomic model out of which compensatory fiscal policy was easily extracted as the means of stabilization in general and recovery from depression in particular.[46]

With the passing years, the Chicagoans' version of balancing the budget over the business cycle evolved as it did, partly owing to the influence of J. M. Clark. Already away from the Midway, Clark had pointed out that equality between savings and "capital expenditures" (the equilibrium condition for the economy) might occur at less than the full employment of labor. Clark talked of aggregate equilibrium in terms of two *simultaneous* "balances"—one between the supply and demand for goods and the other between supply and demand for productive services, especially labor. This was a careful statement of what the Chicagoans tacitly must have assumed all along, inasmuch as they had argued mostly for the stabilization of output *and* employment. Especially after Clark's notion of aggregate equilibrium, it became clear through Paul Douglas's writings that the Chicagoans generally and Douglas particularly wanted to balance the budget at full employment outputs, execute a deficit at less than full employment outputs, and execute a surplus at inflationary (greater than full employment) outputs. In this sense, Paul Douglas's *Controlling Depressions* was a harbinger to the rule of balancing the budget under conditions of high employment, thought first to have been enunciated by H. Christian Sonne and Beardsley Ruml in their National Planning Association pamphlet, *Fiscal and Monetary Policy*, published in 1944. ▓▓

46. J. Ronnie Davis, "Chicago Economists, Deficit Budgets, and the Early 1930s," *American Economic Review*, 58 (June 1968), 476–82.

4

Other Leading Economists

Chicago's Allies

ADDING their voices to the Chicago foray, other economists also argued for expansion. As a matter of fact, another so-called "school" flourished at Columbia, and its devotees in residence, the most notable of whom was J. M. Clark who had switched his allegiance in 1926 from Chicago, demonstrated a growing interest in business cycles. The Columbia economists, closely identified with the equally flourishing National Bureau of Economic Research, did not always articulate the various elements of their theory, and the inordinate amount of measurement without theory must have proved to many to be a stultifying tradition.

Other leading, published economists were expressing themselves on a variety of issues. Wage policy was certainly discussed, but few endorsed wage cutting as an unemployment policy. Most saw in it a threat to aggregate demand. Some economists were initiating interest in and even endorsing panaceas for recovery which were invariably bizarre, embracing everything from economic apartheids for the unemployed to new monetary standards.

J. M. CLARK

During the 1920s one of the premier devotees of business cycle theory and measurement in the United States was John

Maurice Clark, who, to the benefit of the profession, did not limit himself to any particular area of economics. During the early 1930s, Clark produced two remarkable pieces of literature. In one, he turned his attention to the nature of boom and depression, and in the other to the remedy for depression.

In his *Strategic Factors in Business Cycles,* published in 1934, Clark treated everything from cyclical patterns to the meaning and requirements of equilibrium. From the very outset of his study, Clark notably called attention to the accelerator principle, a 1917 discovery of his. Changes in effective demand, viz., purchasing desire *and* purchasing power, were owing to changes in income. Consumption was thus a function of income in Clark's explanation. Changes in aggregate demand and income were related, in turn, to changes in the rate of productive activity. While demand, income, consumption, and the like were dependent upon "business responses," the rate of investment was dependent upon expectations ("prospects of business profits"). Investment demand for capital equipment, moreover, fluctuated more intensely than the output of the goods it served to produce, Clark argued. If fluctuations in income, consumption and saving, output, prices, and employment were to be explained, this accelerator principle was of "peculiar strategic importance." In short:

The total effect is summed up in saying that fluctuations in consumption, or in consumers' current expenditures, are passed on in the form of more intense fluctuations in the producers' expenditures on the durable means of gratifying these consumers' demands; and even changes in the rate of growth of consumption may bring about positive ups and downs in the resulting expenditures of producers. Since each expenditure constitutes someone else's income, the result is a widespread fluctuation of incomes and a corresponding fluctuation in consumers' consequent expenses. Thus slight disturbances are self-multiplying.[1]

A further pattern of interest is Clark's consumption function—a sort of bold, Keynesian formulation. Clark asserted that

1. J. M. Clark, *Strategic Factors in Business Cycles* (New York: National Bureau of Economic Research, 1934), p. 78.

as the national income increases, consumer expenditures increase less rapidly than total income, and savings available for expenditures on producers' goods increase more rapidly. The marginal propensity to consume, to use Keynes's jargon, decreases in cyclical upswings. As Alvin Hansen has pointed out, this is a much less cautious version of the consumption function than Keynes's.[2]

In Clark's model, consumption expenditures were steadier than either production or income. With any given change, consumption would change only a fraction of the change in income. In both the upswing and the downswing, this tended to set a limit to the cumulative effect of a disturbance. That is, a downward trend would be infinite if every reduction of production (hence, income) caused an equal reduction of expenditures. If a reduction of production and income was followed by a smaller reduction of expenditures, however, then the series of derived effects would be a diminishing series with a finite rather than an infinite sum. For example, a contraction of output, hence income, might be followed by a contraction of expenditures only half the size of the former, so that an infinite series of such reductions would only double the amount of the original contraction.

It is interesting to note that Clark's recognition and use of the multiplier principle preceded his seeing Kahn's publication of "Public Works and Inflation."[3] Also interesting is the fact that Clark minimized the strategic importance of consumer expenditures as a control mechanism for manipulating a business cycle. Clark regarded consumer income as a more promising means of manipulation.

It was clear to Clark that business cycles by their very nature were departures from "balance," i.e., equilibrium. This begged the question, however, of what equilibrium is. Clark pointed out that the concept of aggregate equilibrium was weak insofar as it focused only on the approximate equality of supply and

---

2. Alvin H. Hansen, *A Guide to Keynes* (New York: McGraw-Hill, 1953), p. 10.
3. Cf. R. F. Kahn, *Journal of the American Statistical Association*, 27 (March 1933 Supplement), 168–73.

demand for *goods*. The trouble was that "supply and demand for goods may reach momentary balance at very varying levels of price and of volume of production and employment," Clark argued.[4] A more fundamental notion of equilibrium, therefore, must consider equilibrium between supply and demand for *productive forces, especially labor.* Clark deplored the limited, superficial notion of equilibrium as one which embraced only the idea of an equilibrium between the supply and demand for goods. The most serious limitation of this superficial notion was that it ignored the possibility of *underemployment equilibrium.* In Clark's words, "The fact that supply and demand for goods can be balanced at present only at volumes of production that mean an intolerable amount of unemployment (lack of balance between supply and demand for labor) is evidence that the requirements of balance in the superficial [i.e., equilibrium in terms of output] and in the fundamental [i.e., equilibrium in terms of output and productive services, especially labor] senses have not been harmonized, in our present system." (p. 130) An economy in full employment equilibrium, therefore, would exhibit no mismatches of productive powers and productive opportunities, no great discrepancies between supply and demand, and no wastes of productive powers for lack of opportunity to use them. Clark's point was that aggregate equilibrium requires that many things balance simultaneously. "But first and foremost," Clark argued, "we may consider the supply of labor and the volume of employment, recognizing that they are dependent in turn upon a network of conditioning factors which will have to be separately considered." (p. 131)

Balance between the supply and demand for labor, Clark indicated, partially depended on a reasonably steady *rate* of production. Steady production really was nothing more than a corollary of the general assumption of equilbrium between supply and demand. After all, the total supply of labor and capital was relatively steady and could be in equilibrium with demand only when demand absorbed it all. This was theoretically pos-

---

4. Clark, *Strategic Factors*, p. 129. Location of further material quoted from this source is indicated by page numbers in parentheses following the quote.

sible because aggregate demand itself reflected the volume of production and was potentially capable in 1934 of absorbing more goods than yet produced.

From the extreme individualistic standpoint, to which Clark was opposed, fundamental equilibrium amounted to no more than producing the right things, setting prices on them which clear the markets, and adjusting the prices for resources to levels that induce employers to employ them. In other words, if there appeared to be difficulty in maintaining full employment output, prices should not be maintained; if there appeared to be unemployment of labor, wages should not be maintained. Clark was not at all convinced that a country in which extremely individualistic (notably, not classical) policies were actually followed could assure itself of full and steady employment of its productive services.[5] First of all, if wages and prices (and profits) fell by the same amount, Clark indicated, nothing would be accomplished, presumably because real wages (W/P) would be unaffected. Second, if wages did fall more than other shares, the consumer goods market would contract. That is, as income was shifted from wages to profits, the community propensity to consume would decrease and its propensity to save would increase.

Regarding this latter point, Clark advanced a consideration which undermined still further the efficacy of flexible prices and wages in eliminating business cycles. If all savings were spent automatically and promptly as investment expenditures, aggregate demand would be the same regardless of the level of savings, and expenditures would equal the value of production (i.e., Say's Identity would hold). In the Wicksell-Robertson-Myrdal-Keynes tradition, Clark pointed out that this simply did not happen automatically. A number of steps in the process had to balance among themselves if total savings were to equal net expenditures for capital goods. In any number of ways, the people with savings might provide a greater or smaller volume of funds

5. Clark identifies this cult as the "extreme individualists," not the "classical" school. In this sense, Clark was similar to Henry Simons, who objected to Keynes's use of the term "classical" to describe what Simons called "bad applications of traditional theory." Cf. Henry C. Simons, "Keynes Comments on Money," *Christian Century* (22 July 1936), pp. 1016–17.

seeking productive investment than businessmen would want for capital expenditures. Therein lie discrepancies between savings and expenditures for capital goods. In the long run (*ex post*, presumably), there would be "balance." If purchases of capital goods exceeded savings $(I > S)$, the excess of these capital goods would be liquidated out of the greater savings forthcoming from increased income. Since saving and consumption were functions of income, an excess of investment over savings would cause income to increase, ridding the system of the disparity. If savings were not channeled into capital goods $(S > I)$, on the other hand, the planned saving would not remain in existence. Again, since savings is a function of income, an excess of savings over investment would cause a decrease in income, hence savings.[6]

In the last one-third of *Strategic Factors*, Clark turned to an accelerator-multiplier theory of the business cycle as a whole. If factors were grouped into those having to do directly with production and those having to do directly with consumption, it would be impossible to identify one group as the active one and the other as the passive because they would interact so completely. Clark chose to start at the point in the cycle where an excess of savings over investment ("hoarding," with the clear indication that there was nothing to bring into line the separate decisions to save and to invest), and hence a shrinkage of consumers' purchases had occurred. "The basic decline in consumers' purchases is a common feature of all cycles," Clark noted, "and is mainly consequent upon an actual shrinkage in consumers' incomes, resulting in turn from a prior shortage of general employment and lessened production in industries at large." (p. 168)

6. Clark probably was influenced to some extent by Keynes's *Treatise* (cf. Keynes, *A Treatise on Money* [New York: Harcourt, Brace and Co., 1930]). Much earlier, he had pointed out that the connection between stock speculation and the general business cycle was such that investment funds during a depression flow into existing securities rather than into new investment. Money tends to be cheap at such times. "This condition implies that savings are in excess of investment in the Keynes terminology," Clark casually mentioned (cf. Clark, *Strategic Factors*, p. 59). The point here is that Clark had knowledge of the savings-investment disparity thesis which Keynes popularized to the English-speaking world, but which had been developed earlier by Wicksell, Myrdal, and even Robertson.

Why should consumption expenditures decrease? Not because of a wave of savings owing to, say fear of losing jobs, but to a general curtailment of employment and production, which causes the decline of income and which entails decreases in consumer goods production *prior* to the decrease in consumption expenditures. Since capital goods production is partially a function of the rate of consumer goods production, there is consequently a more intensive decline in capital goods production. Total expenditures, therefore, decline by more than consumer expenditures out of current income. In brief, therefore, the Clark mechanism involves (a) change in rate of increase in consumer expenditures, (b) decrease in employment, (c) decrease in incomes, (d) decrease in consumer expenditures, (e) more intensive decrease in investment expenditure, etc.

In more detail, Clark finally admitted that "impulses" lead to up- or down-turns of business. Largely exogenous, these impulses consist of production increases "without waiting for demand;" demand increases for capital goods "without waiting for increased demand for products;" shifts in consumers' demand from one commodity to another such that a "net increase in the demand for equipment" results; or an "upward inflection in the course of total consumers' demand . . . from causes not dependent on prior increase in income (which would have to rest on increased production)." (pp. 174–75) These exogenous increases of demand, not derived from prior increases of production and income, are made possible by expansion of credit (apparently moving in response to demand) and, more importantly, lead to increased productive activity and to increased incomes prior to the time when the consumer output of the new equipment is actually on the markets. The effect of these exogenous increases in demand is an increase in general purchasing power, which in turn both intensifies the exogenous increase and spreads its influence over commodities in general, thus further stimulating the demand for capital.

The conditions of upswing $(I > S)$ cannot endure, however. The increased income, brought about by the quickened pace of economic activity, is not all spent. Some of what is "saved" is not channeled into increased purchases of producers' or consumers' goods. Capital goods production eventually slackens, production declines, income distributions decline, and the decline is thereby diffused and intensified, and the cycle reversed.

What, then, are the causes of business cycles? Clark divided them into three classes: (1) originating factors, (2) business responses controlling the short cycle, and (3) factors responsible for longer trends.

In the first group are included purely exogenous factors such as weather, wars, and other chance disturbances which occur independently of the business cycle. Their causation may be entirely noneconomic, but at any rate, it cannot be traced to conditions within the business cycle. In this sense, however, other exogenous factors also belong to this class. Such factors as the origination (in contrast to the rate of development and exploitation) of new wants, new goods, and new processes or methods of production, while not contingent upon any components within the business cycle, are, for all practical purposes, inescapable. Another factor belonging to the general class of originating causes is shifts in foreign trade arising from causes other than the state of the business cycle in our own country.

These foregoing factors, not being a function of any variable within Clark's model of the business cycle, did not appear to be of great *strategic* importance presumably because there is little that can be done about them. The length, timing, and specific features of business cycles were governed by business responses controlling the short cycle and by factors responsible for longer trends. In terms of the first of these, Clark listed eleven major possibilities which involved mainly accelerator-multiplier characteristics.

The first cited of these "responses" which "controlled" the short cycle was the intensified fluctuations of derived demand for both capital and durable consumers' goods. Also mentioned were price movements and the lack of simultaneous and proportionate change in the price system. The most important movements involved wages and interest burdens, or "overhead" costs in general because it was these which determined and intensified the movements of profits. If money wages (W) and money overhead costs (C) lagged behind price changes, in other words, then the decrease of real wages (W/P) and costs (C/P) in the upswing was a source of derived profits.

Movements of speculative demand for commodities, hence money, were also cited as a contributing cause of short cycles. Moreover, one cumulative cause was the "effect of confidence or the lack of it on speculation, on expansion or contraction of business enterprise and on credit purchases generally, including those of consumers." (p. 188) In other words, expectations tended to influence investment expenditures and borrowing decisions in general.

Next, there was an endogenous factor, the dependence of consumers' demand on the level of income. As a function of income, consumption combined with other factors to form a sort of vicious circle which tended to reinforce itself cumulatively. Closely related to this factor was another, changes in the income distribution between different classes and income groups, given the diverse habits and standards of consumption and savings of these groups. This factor was responsible for a degree of instability in the saved and consumed proportions of national income beyond that which arose from simple changes in per capita real income.

His final factor was an important one. Clark maintained that discrepancies between total income and total spendings, which is also to say between savings and investment, were responsible for stimulating expansion and enforcing contraction, depending on the respective magnitudes. Clark was particularly concerned with the extent to which the flexibility of credit encouraged these discrepancies. Extreme credit flexibility enabled other forces to initiate changes in rates of expenditures and production with a freedom not otherwise possible and acted at times as an independent force to stimulate expansion or enforce contraction.

If these were the factors which allowed the originating causes to amass cumulatively to the point of triggering serious departures from fundamental equilibrium, what were the possibilities of controlling them? Factors which were least amenable to control could be dismissed first. These included those associated with business confidence and the consumer's freedom to choose what he wants to do with his income. Of basic importance, however, was coping with the tendency toward intensified fluctuations of derived demand. In other words, the problem was one of controlling investment and its intensifier, the accelerator-multiplier effects. If this tendency could be controlled, the average rate of productive activity could be stabilized by preventing those fluctuations of production which exceeded fluctuations of current consumers' expenditures and the latter themselves would be far more stable.

Clark pondered the possibilities of privately controlling investment and accelerator-multiplier effects, but he came to the conclusion that, while these factors were *potentially* subject to control, control could be achieved only by means of measures which the United States seemed unprepared at that time to take.

But there was always the possibility of using public works, Clark argued. In terms understandably akin to the University of Chicago economists, Clark maintained that if private activity expanded too intensely, public works expenditures could contract; and if private activity contracted, public works expenditures could expand. In short, because public works were inherently amenable to control, they could be used to "neutralize" private movements. Such a policy could not succeed, however, if it consisted exclusively of concentrating *normal* public works in dull times. Such a policy could succeed only as part of a sufficiently larger program, Clark declared.

If a policy of compensatory public spending were undertaken, Clark continued, the method of financing was vitally important because of its effect on the movements of total purchasing power. Not automatically ruling out a net increase in purchasing power, he nevertheless noted that financing by means of taxes generally operates to decrease private expenditures and neutralize the stimulating effect which expanded public works expenditures have on total economic activity. On the other hand, financing by means of credit tends to give public works their maximum effect on the economy. Typical of the public works advocates of this pre-Keynesian period, Clark went on to argue that repayment of public debt should be made insofar as possible in times of active business when restraint was needed. One presumes that Clark intended the bulk of the borrowing and re-payment to involve the Federal Reserve system, in order to avoid the stimulating effect that debt retirement otherwise would have.

Clark admitted that his *Strategic Factors* was not the place to discuss the whole notion of public works. In the following year, however, Clark published a study which he had made for the National Planning Boards of the Federal Emergency Ad-ministration of Public Works.[7] Clark talked here of "a com-pensated economy," as Walter Lippmann called it. By this was meant a government which compensated for rather than directly controlled the evils or disasters wrought by free enterprise. Un-der such a system government would spend more money on public works at a time when business was spending too little, and less money on public works at a time when business was spending too much.

What was meant by "public works"? Normally by that term, one primarily meant fixed structures produced by government. Under serious enough conditions, however, Clark thought enlarg-ing the notion of public works to the extent which would be effective, and thus including perishable services as well as durable goods, was entirely justifiable.

As an antidote to depressions, public works had only a brief history, in terms both of conceptual formulation and actual use. As commonly done, Clark traced the idea to the turn of the century. The minority report of the British Poor Law Com-mission had advocated a scheduling of regular public works and other purchases as a regulator of aggregate economic activity, and this idea had been adopted officially by France as early as 1902. In England, on the other hand, it really was not even tried until 1920–21, by which time the problem was no longer the mild, cyclical fluctuations contemplated by the Webbs. In-stead, this was the beginning of a period of chronic unemploy-ment.

---

7. J. M. Clark, *Economics of Planning Public Works* (Washington, D.C.: United States Government Printing Office, 1935). Location of further material cited from this source is indicated by page numbers in parentheses following the material.

In the United States anticyclical timing of public works had been endorsed officially in 1921 by the President's Conference on Unemployment and actually was executed during the earliest stages of the Depression by President Hoover. The trouble was that the Depression well exceeded the mild fluctuations to which the Webbs addressed themselves. Also, unreasonable pressure had been exerted on governments to reduce current expenses and balance the budget. It seemed incongruous to expand expenditures and employment of one part of the budget and to contract expenditures and employment of others (as President Roosevelt was doing). This created a problem, Clark indicated before treating such matters in detail, which needed to be explained in order to promote confidence that the expansion of public works represented a real increase of public spending fitted into a harmonious and consistent budgetary program.

The first and most obvious general characteristic of shorter business cycles was the movement of prices. This factor, however, only served to transmit underlying causes. Along with changes in prices and, of course, volumes of production went changes in total national income, but the latter affected income shares differently. Business profits demonstrated very intense changes, for example, but wages did not fluctuate as much. Accordingly, the growth of profits in a boom represented purchasing power not fully spent (i.e., it becomes increasingly difficult for investment to exceed savings). Clark's point was that consumers' spending could not increase as fast as the aggregate dollar volume of production. Although he declined the opportunity to develop fully the effects of shifts in the distribution of income, he nonetheless concluded that whereas changes in income distribution and corresponding changes in the proportion of income actually spent played an important part in business cycles, attempts to control the cycles through altering the distribution of spending power were difficult and often beleaguered with effects tending to defeat the end in view.

Again, Clark turned to his accelerator principle when noting that the most intense fluctuations, both in terms of production and prices, occurred in durable goods industries, including construction and fixed capital investment in general. Whether it was the purchase of new goods or the replacement of old ones, investment depended on expectations as well as on more substantial factors. The most serious feature of the accelerator principle, therefore, was that it brought about a corresponding expansion and contraction of general purchasing power, which increased and decreased the total demand for all goods durable and nondurable alike. In this way, the effect of the accelerator was transmitted cumulatively to business in general. The intensified fluctuations in capital goods, in other words, operated to implement a vicious spiral of decreased production and decreased spending power in times of depression.

Changes in investment were the strategic cause of booms and depressions, Clark asserted. Consumers' spending could not be observed to initiate a business expansion or a business contraction. Spending was simply a function of income, and a general decline in incomes typically resulted from a decline in production.

Movements of credit, like changes in consumer spending, were not considered by Clark to be initiating causes of cyclical fluctuations. Instead, movements of credit responded to demands made on credit institutions by expanding or contracting business. What movements of credit did do, however, was *facilitate* expansions and intensify both expansions and contractions. Relating this to the tendency for capital expenditures to expand faster than either consumers' expenditures or incomes during a revival, Clark maintained that, without credit, capital expenditures would be limited to consumer saving of current incomes, which is to say that cumulative expansions hardly could take place at all. An elasticity of credit, on the other hand, meant that expenditures could increase faster than incomes, these expenditures giving rise in turn to increased incomes and so, for a time at least, to still further expansions of spending, etc. (p. 35)

In the theory of public works this proposition could not be ignored as part of fiscal policy. "It is only so far as the funds of public works came either out of credit expansion (or a reduction of credit contraction) or out of individual incomes which would otherwise be saved and not invested in the production of actual productive equipment," Clark indicated, "that a public works program can really have a stimulative effect on the total volume of business." (p. 36) In modern jargon, the stimulative effect can come only from deficit-financed public works or from a balanced budget multiplier.

Finally, Clark turned to the "conjectural movements in relative volumes of savings and investment and related quantities" and advanced the notion of a savings-investment disparity. Although he admittedly had no empirical evidence as yet to support his case, Clark maintained that savings increased during prosperity, but capital expenditures increased faster; and savings shrank during business recessions, but capital expenditures shrank more sharply. During a boom, capital outlays came at least partly out of credit expansion, while during a recession, savings were not spent fully.

The beginning of a decline, then, was not traceable to an initial decline in consumers' spendings. It was caused instead by, variously put, a shortage of investment relative to saving (i.e., I < S), an excess of incomes over spendings, or an excess of productive capacity over total purchasing power. On the other hand, the cause of movements toward recession was the same—a decline in investment. What could public works do to combat such a decline? Clark maintained that public works could compensate for the deficiency in private demand, reducing its magnitude by reducing its cumulative effects.

Suppose that aggregate consumers' purchasing power were supplemented by government spending as rapidly as private sources of income declined. Aggregate demand would be maintained. If productive capacity were competent to satisfy this demand, on the other hand, private investment would decline until replacements or new capital equipment were forthcoming. Until such time as private investment recovered to some extent, the burden of filling the deflationary gap would fall exclusively on public expenditures. What public works could do, therefore, was forestall a decline in the production of consumers' goods, and thereby, the intensified decline in private demand for producers' goods.

In Clark's judgment, aggregate production, public and private, could be maintained at peak levels only if government (1) expanded its expenditures during depressed periods and did not simply shift them from prosperous to depressed periods, and (2) financed this expansion in such a way that the funds did not come out of private incomes which otherwise would be spent. For the short run, the latter could be accomplished by inflationary borrowing, but for the long run, Clark thought that its success depended on the discovery of forms of taxation which did not draw upon funds which would be spent (say, a steeply progressive income tax or a tax on savings).

Recession as a process consisted, in summary, of general declines: first in production, next in incomes, and finally in consumer spending. Mild recessions typically were marked by a cessation of credit expansion, but not by the absolute contraction in the volume of bank credit which typically accompanied severe business contractions. The evidence indicated that such declines could be neither checked nor reversed merely by offering credit more freely. Something had to be done to make the market absorb more credit, "to create an effective demand for it." (p. 39) In other words, industrial expansion had to be promoted, for expanding industries constituted the source of effective demand for credit.

Here was where a public works program fitted into the picture. Public expenditures, especially for construction, acted directly to increase the flow of purchasing power. "And the Government is in a position, at such a time, to use its credit to raise funds for such a purpose," Clark maintained, "and so, in part at least, to make up for the failure of private industry to use all the credit which the banking institutions have available at such times." (p. 39) Insofar as purchasing power was concerned, in other words, public capital expenditures would have the same effect as private capital expenditures. Also, a multiplier effect came about when the people who received these public expenditures proceeded to spend their incomes.

In commenting on progressive changes within the economy which might be contributing to cyclical disturbances, Clark evaluated the merits of the theory concerning oversaving as a rationale for a generous program of public expenditures. This theory advanced the notion that a prosperous country tended to save too much of its income. The inexorable result was a productive capacity greatly exceeding the output which consumers were able and willing to take off markets. The function of public works was to increase public spending and to finance it out of national income which otherwise would have been saved and invested in surplus facilities for private production. Clark was not impressed. Oversaving was harmless as long as this saving was spent in ways that created employment and hence enhanced incomes. The trouble developed when further savings were not spent. "It appears, then," Clark indicated, "that the direct source of the trouble lies in a shortage of investment rather than an excess of savings in and of itself." (p. 47) Time and time again, Clark returned to the point that changes in investment were the root cause of departures from fundamental equilibrium.

Clark went on to dismiss the role of the interest rate in equating saving and investment. First, he pointed out the influence of expectations on investment, maintaining that "fairly high rates of interest do not deter business from overinvestment in prosperous times, nor do low rates of interest suffice in themselves to raise investment to normal figures in dull times when the prospect of profits from additional investment has vanished." (p. 48) Second, Clark denied that saving was a function of the interest rate, contending that "changed interest rates, within the usual range of such changes, do not have any great effect in stimulating or retarding savings." (p. 48) As a matter of fact, considering that lowering the interest rate appreciated outstanding securities, changed interest rates might work against the effect that is required to bring about equilibrium. In short, Clark affirmed that the interest rate could not be counted on to bring about equilibrium between savings and investment.

Returning more directly to public works themselves, Clark commented on some of the difficulties of a countercyclical public spending program. More interesting than his commentary on the largely political obstacles was Clark's discussion of expansion of public spending without a subsequent contraction. The oversavings theory, which Clark had claimed was really an underinvestment theory, had proposed a continuing increase in the average rate of public spending to offset the consistent tendency of a prospering country to save more and more of its national income. This view held that the proper role of public spending was to provide not compensatory but secular increases. In other words, it held that the proper role of public works was "to absorb permanently an increased amount of the spending and producing power of the country in order to correct an enduring tendency to maldistribution of effort." (p. 67) Using the terminology of the stagnation thesis cult, Clark continued that "according to this theory the real source of stagnation, or the more serious source, lies deeper than temporary bursts of expansion of capital facilities which proceed in excess of current savings and are financed largely by credit expansion." (p. 67) In still other words, Clark reiterated that "this real source of trouble is held to lie in a persistent tendency of savings to expand faster than industry can absorb them in useful forms of capital equipment, consistent with a stable and healthy industrial development." (pp. 67–68)

Did Clark agree that the average flow of savings tended to exceed private investment? He did, but at the same time admitted that the evidence for this proposition was really insufficient. Clark proposed a very large initial expansion of public works financed by inflationary borrowing and, next, a permanent enlargement of public spending financed by taxation levied primarily on incomes which otherwise would not be spent. Clark hedged a bit on the latter, because of his doubt surrounding the efficacy of either taxes on saving or steeply progressive income taxes in contributing substantial increments to revenue without reducing private spending.

By the time of this writing Clark had a chance to consider more carefully the multiplier effects of public expenditures. In his 1934 *Strategic Factors* he discussed the multiplier at some length, but he had not yet seen R. F. Kahn's articles. Now, a year after *Strategic Factors*, Clark devoted a chapter to the cumulative effects of public expenditures.

Clark classified the employment created by public works as follows:

Primary: (a) Direct, i.e., employment of workers on the spot in carrying out the work; (b) indirect, i.e., employment in producing materials and delivering them to the site of the work and in other services contributing to the work.

Secondary: Employment resulting from the expenditures of all those among whom the original public outlays are divided as income. This includes wage earners and receivers of rent, interest, and profits, since a given dollar of public works expenditures goes to all those varieties of ultimate recipients. (p. 80)

Clark frankly admitted that secondary employment and secondary volume of expenditures were difficult to estimate. He nonetheless cited two possible methods of measuring them: (1) the successive-spendings approach, and (2) the volume and velocity of circulating medium approach. Clark focused on the former, which is the approach that has survived.

The successive-spendings approach was based on the assumption that, given the net contribution of government to aggregate spending, "only a certain part of it is respent by the recipient in ways which go to increase industrial activity within that same community." (p. 85) Of that fraction, only a fraction is spent; etc. "If the fraction remained the same through these successive cycles (as it presumably would not do)," Clark indicated, "then the result of the original spending by Government would be an endless series of further spendings, dwindling in size in such a way that the total sum to infinity would be a definite and finite quantity." (p. 85) By illustration, then, Clark demonstrated that the multiplier was the reciprocal of the fraction not respent, i.e., the marginal propensity to save.

Clark stated, however, that no mechanical formula could do justice to the many variables which affected the multiplier. In brief, he cited several conditions which the mechanical formula tacitly assumed to hold. Mainly, the expenditures had to be inflationary by which Clark and others meant that the expenditures had to represent an addition to and not a transfer of spending. The attempt to estimate the secondary effects of public expenditures depended first, therefore, on the question, "How much of the expenditure on public works is inflationary?" (p. 86) To this question, Clark suggested that "in a strongly marked depression, funds spent for public works will be borrowed, and the borrowings will not take capital which would otherwise be used by industry." (p. 86) During such periods, more savings are offered than industry is willing or able to invest. As the economy recovers, however, this becomes less and less true. Nevertheless, contrary to such a notion, in 1935 banks still had large surplus reserves.

A second question in estimating secondary effects was "How long is the cycle from the spending of increased money income by an ultimate recipient to the next resulting spending of increased income by the next ultimate recipient?" (p. 86) Clark had no real insights into this issue, and he focused instead on a third question, "How great are the 'leakages' representing uses of this money which do not, or do not immediately, result in a stimulus to the actual volume of production?" (p. 86)

The leakages which weakened the multiplier were myriad. Amounts spent for imported goods constituted one leakage. A more important leakage was savings (also, repayment of debt, liquidation of inventories, and replenishment of weakened reserves), which, in a period of depression, had no effect at all in stimulating actual capital. Another leakage was "the amount of this added purchasing power which is absorbed in increasing prices rather than increasing the volume of production and real incomes." (p. 89) The effect of the public expenditures on private capital expenditures was still another conjectural factor.

Somewhat in the spirit of review, Clark spent the last several pages considering prevailing fiscal policy and proposals for reform. He firmly dissented from the two-budget notion on grounds that the cutting of "normal" expenditures to balance the current budget just made the job of the "emergency" budget more difficult. Clark thought that the principle of contracting one budget while expanding another could not be the proper basis for an enduring fiscal policy.

Clark also reiterated that public expenditures were stimulative only to the extent that they represented a net addition to aggregate expenditures. Enlarged public expenditures financed by increased taxation would have a limited effect. Insofar as income taxes reduced savings rather than spendings, in other words, public spending financed by income taxes would have some stimulative effect. Here is the germ of the balanced budget multiplier. The most clearly stimulative form of financing was public borrowing which came out of the expansive power of the credit system rather than out of the savings of individuals.

Clark concluded that the stimulative effect of a public works program was not assured merely by expanding public works. The effect of public works programs, Clark argued, "depends upon how they are financed, or what is happening to the entire budget of public expenditures, and on the effect which these public expenditures produce upon the field for private capital investment and upon the supply of funds available for private capital expenditures." (p. 89)

J. M. Clark was a frontiersman of the profession. He developed an elaborate theory, based on multiplier and accelerator principles, which explained the relationships between investment, production, income, spending, and saving. He made consumption and saving functions of income, and investment largely a function of expectations. Clark pointed out that disparities between savings and investment had cumulative effects on income, and he argued that the interest rate could not equilibrate savings and investment. If anything could, it was income. Clark pointed out that there could be underemployment equilibrium, and he advanced the notion of full employment equilibrium, "balance" in output and input markets. He denied that an economy left to its own forces would cure itself of depression. He argued that a cut in money wages would leave real wages unaffected if prices fell commensurately. Clark found redress of unemployment in fiscal policy and explicitly not in monetary policy. He identified changes in investment as the strategic factor in causing depression and boom, and he proposed changes in public spending as the key to offsetting these private fluctuations.

It is commonly admitted that Clark was a harbinger to Keynes, with the qualification, however, that he did not piece together or offer a comprehensive theory analogous to the *General Theory*. The fact is that Clark built a theory of aggregates within the context of an explanation of business cycles. And he built this theory on building blocks not dissimilar to those Keynes later used in his own theory. The differences were actually few, but important. Keynes developed a theory which at times seemed to be designed solely to buttress his policy proposals. Clark's unwillingness to synthesize the various elements of his theory made it extremely difficult to test or to apply. The formulation of individual propositions exclusive of a comprehensive theory was as stultifying as a general theory devoid of specific points. Economists from Columbia and the National Board of Economic Research—including Clark—simply failed to integrate plausible propositions into a verifiable model.

J. W. SUNDELSON

To Clark's substantial study of public works was appended J. Wilner Sundelson's "Fiscal Aspects of Planned Public Works."[8] At this time a graduate student at Columbia, Sundelson contributed still another articulate recommendation in support of a compensatory role of government.

First of all, Sundelson thought it crucial to recall that, until recently, the relationships between fiscal activities and the general economy had been considered insignificant. It was understandable to him that the mainstream of public finance literature had failed for so long to concern itself with these interactions and the problems they raised. After all, history illustrated only small volumes of government expenditures, both relatively and absolutely. Fiscal scientists naturally were aware of a steady growth of the public sector, but they did not concern themselves with conditions which might arise after increases in the dimensions of fiscal activity had continued for some time. Sundelson also found other explanations for the lack of concern over these fiscal-macroeconomic relationships in the *laissez faire* body of

8. Ibid., pp. 169–94. Sundelson explained that his preliminary findings and conclusions were prepared during June 1934 and revised in August of that year. The research which led to his report apparently was part of a more extended study that he planned to release in the fall of 1934. His efforts were diverted to other purposes, however, and he was unable to complete his more ambitious study. Accordingly, Sundelson's appended report represented preliminary findings and conclusions which, according to him, might have been amplified.

economic theory and the failure of some political economists to consider money operations a significant factor. At any rate, even the public finance theories which once had influenced and molded fiscal legislation failed to analyze the relationships existing between the state and the economy. For example, Sundelson said, taxes are seldom criticized or defended because of the effects which they might have on the economy in general.

Sundelson argued that whatever the reasons for having ignored them in the past, inattention to fiscal-macroeconomic relationships could not continue in the face of the severity of cyclical fluctuations, as evidenced in the Depression. Such experience made it imperative that steps be taken to eliminate any contribution of the fiscal system toward accentuating the Depression. In particular, the success of the fiscal system in dealing with seasonal fluctuations encouraged confidence that it might also successfully cope with cyclical fluctuations.[9] The fiscal policy that Sundelson had in mind involved cyclically balancing the budget, which, according to him, was a frequently advocated policy.

Sundelson complained that policy choice during depression commonly was based on faulty reasoning. "In terms of recovery objectives," he argued, "a creation of new purchasing power generally, and the stimulation of heavy durable goods industries specifically, seems to be desirable."[10] Taxation would result mostly in a shifting of available purchasing power and could not exercise the same type of influence which borrowing and credit expansion could exert.

In Sundelson's judgment, no effective public works program could rely on postponement or retardation of normal expenditures. It was necessary instead to think in terms of a program involving several billions of dollars, and, according to him, it was extremely unlikely that anticyclical timing of public works could be counted on. During future depressions, as a matter of fact, Sundelson foresaw a growing use of debt for maintenance of current services. Like J. M. Clark, Sundelson

9. Sundelson saw a noteworthy beginning in the multiple budget policy allowing balancing of the current budget and borrowing for the extraordinary budget, which was linked specifically to initiating recovery.
10. Ibid., p. 179.

charged that deflation in a current budget in order to facilitate
the financing of an extraordinary budget was hardly a sound
recovery measure.

In juxtaposition with Clark's text, Sundelson's appendix
on the fiscal aspects of public works really did not add a great
deal. What it mainly did was to add still another name to the
already large and growing list of economists who were agitating
for government action, in the way of expansionary fiscal policy,
to end the Depression.

ARTHUR D. GAYER: THE NATIONAL PLANNING BOARD AGAIN

During the same year that Clark's report for the National
Planning Board was published, Arthur D. Gayer's report, *Public
Works in Prosperity and Depression,* was also published.[11] In his
study, this Columbia economist presented the history of the
concept of utilizing planned public works as a stabilizer and
traced the applications of it at local, state, and federal levels of
government. More important for the purpose here, he discussed
at some length the financing of public works and some problems surrounding the use of public works as a stabilizer.

If public spending were expanded (or maintained at high
levels) during depression, Gayer broached, the financing must
be mainly through borrowing. The budget could be unbalanced
through steady increases in expenditures while revenues were
declining, or the "emergency expenditures" and debt could be
segregated into an extraordinary budget. Either way, large issues
of bonds were necessary. "Though long advocated for the purpose," Gayer pointed out, "only during the recent depression was
an attempt made on a large scale to stimulate business and alle-
viate unemployment by accelerating and expanding public construction." (p. 268)

In much the same way that J. M. Clark and P. H. Douglas

11. Arthur D. Gayer, *Public Works in Prosperity and Depression* (New York:
National Bureau of Economic Research, 1935). Location of further material
quoted from this source is indicated by page numbers in parentheses following
the quote.

identified the culprit, Gayer argued that recession occurred when private investment decreased *absolutely* or *relatively*. "[T]he recession is characterized," Gayer explained in definite Clarkian fashion, "by a falling off of production in capital and other durable goods industries, by attendant unemployment, by a decrease in total consumers' incomes, by consequent contracted demand for consumption goods, by more unemployment, by less production, and so on." (p. 350) In identifying the culprit as the investment-production-employment-income-consumption nexus, Gayer rightly claimed no originality. He claimed that "the heart of the problem of business fluctuation has long been recognized to lie in this rise and fall of investment in new capital goods, both producers' goods and durable consumers' goods." (p. 368)

Gayer flatly denied that monetary weapons alone could restore aggregate purchasing power during periods of recession. Availability of funds for investment "will not induce [new investment] so long as the prospective rate of profit on it is likely to be a minus quantity," Gayer indicated. (p. 369) A flexible program of public works as an application of the compensatory fiscal policy was needed, he concluded. Gayer also explicitly rejected the notion that public borrowing and spending merely diverted resources from the private sector, thereby failing to create any additional employment. "Since, however, there is usually during depression periods a surplus of idle funds seeking secure investment at attractive returns, which private industry is unable or unwilling to utilize," Gayer maintained, "its use by public bodies need not necessarily involve transference of spending power from private enterprise, inasmuch as this capital might otherwise not have been employed at all." (p. 376)

Again under the influence of J. M. Clark, Gayer argued that an expansion of government expenditures accompanied by expansion of credit would create additional means of payment and employment, and hence, increased consumer and producer demand. In short, then, Gayer was submitting that businessmen are reluctant in recession periods to make capital expenditures in the face of uncertainty, declining costs, and excessive productive capacity; that investment funds are likely to remain idle as unemployed bank, personal, and corporate balances; that it is from these reservoirs of credit that the means to finance expanded public works largely can be drawn; and finally that this need cause no diversion of resources.

Gayer then returned to his argument that monetary policy was impotent. Making money cheap via a low rediscount rate might not have the desired effect of creating bank deposits and increasing consumer buying and producer borrowing. There simply was no guarantee that sound borrowers would come forward automatically. Business activity did not depend on making borrowing easier or cheaper. In a depression, the encouragement of business activity "depends upon whether business men consider they can increase production profitably, and that in turn depends largely upon the probable future volume of demand and the trend of prices." (p. 376) If private investment depended on the question of profits, actual or prospective, then making borrowing easier or cheaper would not guarantee success at all.

Gayer was supporting the argument that credit expansion is best achieved through a public works program sufficiently large to ensure that the additional credit made available will be spent. Expenditures of large amounts, Gayer continued, accounted for jobs to the idle both directly and to a greater extent indirectly, and also stimulated production.

Gayer also denied the validity of two other objections to deficit-financed public works. First, he denied that the debt involved a future increased burden of taxation. To the contrary, he contended, recovery brings with it increased tax receipts without additional taxation. The point was that prosperity could not be just around the corner if everyone, including governments, was spending progressively less and less. Second, he minimized the charge of inevitable waste. If any waste did occur, it would be negligible relative to the economic waste of idle labor and capital. Besides, Gayer continued, the real net direct cost of public works was far less than the gross cost, because of the decrease in subsidies to the unemployed as well as the increase in tax receipts from increased incomes. The apparent magnitude of the initial cost was deceptive because of the "secondary" effects of flexible public works expenditures.

His discussion of the secondary effects of public spending showed that Gayer clearly grasped the notion of the multiplier and that, not surprisingly, he followed Clark's version of the multiplier principle rather than, say, Keynes's or Kahn's. Gayer, following Clark's terminology, identified the employment of workers on public projects as the "direct primary" effect and the employment of workers in producing and transporting construction materials as the "indirect primary" effects of public spending. When the increased purchasing power resulting from the additional aggregate incomes received by those engaged in the publicly financed employments was manifested in increased demand for goods, this created still further employment which Gayer called "secondary employment."

Just as Douglas and Clark had done earlier, Gayer pointed out that, because of leakages, the effects of public spending did not multiply indefinitely. "Some of the added income will be saved, some will merely be a substitute for previous expenditure by private charity, some will be used to pay off old debts, . . . some of the increased income might also be spent on imports, or raise prices and thus diminish consumption, unless producers spend their increased profits," Gayer suggested. (p. 386) Gayer then concluded by citing Keynes's calculation of the multiplier as it appeared in *The Means to Prosperity*.

There was little in Gayer's treatise which others (e.g., Douglas and Clark) had not already said. His meager contribution does help to demonstrate, however, that here was still another leading economist who fails to fit well into the "classical" mold. Gayer had a firm grasp of macroeconomic relationships involving investment, production, employment, income, and consumption, and he had little trouble in seeing the remedy to conditions which depressed these functions.

CANNING AND NELSON

John B. Canning and E. G. Nelson, two Stanford University economists, were also among those who began in the early 1930s to crusade for a compensatory fiscal policy. In 1934 they counted themselves among the advocates of the idea that balancing the budget over the business cycle would tend to stabilize private economic activity, which they suggested was currently a much advocated proposition.

It was Canning's and Nelson's argument that the budget policy of restricting the annual volume of operations to the annual revenue yield had never been and never could be a permanent government policy. Contrariwise, the purpose of budgets was not to constrain financial programs, but to insure advance planning of both expenditure and revenue activities. "If the government is to use its peculiar facilities to counterbalance excesses in private enterprise," therefore, "it must plan for the acceleration of economic activity in periods of depression and for restraint upon such activities in times of prosperity," they maintained.[12] Such a program clearly would forbid annual budget balancing and require the adjustment of revenue and expenditure over the business cycle.

Canning and Nelson were simply arguing that sensible fiscal policy required government to plan and adjust tax rates or levels of expenditure according to business conditions. "In periods of depression [the government] might lower tax rates, borrow heavily, and increase public expenditure," they argued, and "in terms of prosperity it must tax at higher rates, reduce expenditures, and decrease the public debt."[13]

The remainder of the Canning and Nelson paper was devoted to the description of a mode of measuring taxable income and to establishing the objectives which tax policy should promote. They made it clear that one of the primary objectives which their system must attain was a countercyclical Treasury policy. "If year-by-year budget balancing is abandoned," they maintained, "the Treasury can throw the weight of its borrowing and lending operations and of its revenue collections and disbursements as dampers against the successive booms and depressions which we may otherwise expect."[14]

12. John B. Canning and E. G. Nelson, "The Relation of Budget Planning to Economic Stabilization: A Suggested Federal Treasury Policy," *American Economic Review*, 24 (March 1934), 27.
13. Ibid., pp. 27–28.
14. Ibid., p. 36.

ARTHUR R. BURNS

In May 1935 A. R. Burns, also at Columbia, was arguing that increased production could be sustained only if aggregate spending were increased. In regard to this end of increasing spending, he moderately praised the intentions of the National Recovery Administration insofar as it operated to augment employment, purchasing power, and income, but he complained about the government's own policy of wage cutting, which, along with raising prices, neutralized such effects. Burns also had moderate praise for the monetary policy of the Roosevelt administration. Purchases of securities by the Federal Reserve banks and liberalization of the law controlling the issuance of currency, however, had served only to increase excess reserves of member banks. There simply remained an unwillingness to borrow in spite of very low interest rates, Burns pointed out.

The most encouraging recovery agent was a public works program, Burns concluded. "This policy commends itself because it is a proposal for actual spending by the government," he argued, "and because it directs the additional spending to the industries in which there is the greatest proportion of unused resources, namely the durable producers goods industries."[15] Burns explicitly pointed out, moreover, that public works stimulated recovery only insofar as they increased aggregate spending. They might, however, have other consequences which would tend to neutralize their stimulative effect. For example, the government borrowing necessary to finance public works might discourage private borrowing and spending by raising the rate of interest.

Burns also was concerned that enlarged government spending might have to be *secular,* owing to the possibility that the increased production resulting from public works expenditures could be maintained only by continuing such expenditures. His misgivings arose out of his awareness that a widespread fear of secular spending might pose an obstacle to recovery.

15. Arthur R. Burns, "Discussion," *Journal of Farm Economics,* 17 (May 1935), 255–56.

In short, Burns argued that the private sector was decreasingly effective in fully employing the means of production. Although less clearly than Douglas or Clark, Burns saw in the savings-investment disparity a problem, and he went on to say that "the interest rate operates very unsatisfactorily as a regulator of saving and investment."[16] At any rate, Burns was convinced that departures from full employment were so great during depression as to make government intervention to relieve unemployment and stimulate production impossible to avoid. The pressure was unmistakably there, Burns asserted, for government to stimulate production. Then, in clear recognition of the possibility of unemployment equilibrium, Burns concluded that "without effective intervention to stimulate recovery, production may attain a relatively stable equilibrium without full utilization of resources."[17]

R. V. SWIFT

In mid-1934 R. V. Swift was typical of economists trying to estimate the impact of public works expenditures on such important variables as employment. Associated with the Commercial Department of the Illinois Bell Telephone Company, Swift wanted to estimate how many would be employed, directly and indirectly, by the Public Works Administration. Swift noted that a widely accepted estimate of employment in construction industries was that made by Keynes in his *Means to Prosperity* (1933). Although Keynes, being a strong advocate of vigorous public works spending, was unlikely to underestimate the indirect employment, Swift declared that he was willing nonetheless to use Keynes's estimate.

A further concern associated with the determination of derived employment was the method of financing public expenditures. "Where idle financial resources were used for a construction program such as that of the Public Works Administration,"

16. Ibid., p. 258.
17. Ibid.

Swift argued, "no decrease in employment and production in private industry should result."[18] The same was true if the expenditures were financed out of a net increase in bank credit, he contended. An increase in taxes, on the other hand, would likely take some funds from industry that might have been used for private business expansion.

SOME OTHERS

There were others saying essentially the same sort of thing. This does not suggest an answer to the question as to how many strictly independent ideas had gone into the mix. To illustrate a point, there is a story of a group of GNP forecasters in government (plus one or two from universities) which met in Washington about once a month from 1945–55 to discuss business conditions and to exchange forecasts. When asked how many "degrees of freedom" lay behind the group's mean monthly forecast, one of them answered slightly facetiously that his estimate was "One!"

In the March 1933 Supplement to the *Journal of the American Statistical Association,* at any rate, two articles were published which echoed much of the above. In one, J. Douglas Brown of Princeton University pointed out the obvious—that appeals to employers had been ineffective in stimulating employment—and argued that experience led increasingly to the judgment that governmental loans and expenditures were a necessary stimulus to new employment. Stimulation of the construction industry was the chief objective, according to Brown, and governmental spending of "huge sums" on "construction of highways, public buildings, and other improvements was demanded by a great majority of economists and public-minded citizens."[19] Later, by the way, Brown endorsed "barter exchanges" for the unemployed, a panacea sponsored by Frank D. Graham.

18. R. V. Swift, "The Employment Possibilities of the Federal Public Works Fund," *Journal of Business of the University of Chicago,* 7 (July 1934), 260.
19. J. Douglas Brown, "The Scientific Stimulation of Employment," *Journal of the American Statistical Association,* 28 (March 1933 Supplement), 174–78.

In the same issue of the *Journal of the American Statistical Association,* Corrington Gill also agreed that the construction industry was the chief point of attack.[20] A federal government administrator closely associated with the WPA, Gill argued that the practical method of preventing extreme cyclical fluctuations within the construction industry consisted in advanced planning of public works. His plea was for countercyclical public spending and the advance planning or approval of expenditure programs which he thought necessary to mitigate seemingly inherent lags in the decision making of the Congress and the Executive.

Other Themes

Most of the discussion heretofore has focused largely on fiscal policy and only incidentally on monetary policy. Little has been said, except in passing, about the wage policy literature, about the panaceas sponsored by leading economists, or about the contractionist literature. These remaining themes are, each in its own way, important in delineating the particulars, if not the climate, of classical intraprofessional opinon.

WAGE POLICY

Wage policy was discussed widely in the pre-Keynesian years of the Depression. The discussion was due largely to the pervasive wage cutting in the private sector and, particularly during the Roosevelt Administration, in the public sector as well. From the very outset of the 1930s, leading pre-Keynesian economists in the United States do not appear to have endorsed wage reductions as the key to augmenting the volume of employment. Contrariwise, most of them appear to have opposed wage cutting quite vigorously if they thought opposition was needed at all.

20. Corrington Gill, "The Effectiveness of Public Works in Stabilizing the Construction Industry," *Journal of the American Statistical Association,* 28 (March 1933 Supplement), 199.

Would one really expect the "classical" school to have proposed wage policy as the solution to fluctuations in employment? Had they believed in cutting wages to offset unemployment during depression, these economists with such a strong penchant for symmetry (as evidenced in their insistence on balancing the budget over the business cycle) undoubtedly would have prescribed wage increases to provide unemployment during boom periods. This was unheard of, of course.

Allyn A. Young keynoted the American "classical" economists' attitude toward wage policy as early as 1929. In that edition of the *Encyclopaedia Britannica,* Young challenged Say's Law in his article, "Supply and Demand." To view aggregate supply and aggregate demand merely as different aspects of a single situation was to Young an oversimplification which led to mistaken conclusions, one being that general overproduction is impossible. It was obvious to Young that production could either exceed or fall short of an expansion of money incomes. In his article on wages, Young went on to deny that a general wage reduction would lead to increased employment of labor in a way similar to the case where a reduction of the price of a particular commodity leads to larger sales. In so doing, Young rejected the wisdom of wage cuts in periods of recession.

At about the same time, Paul Douglas was arguing that unemployment caused by seasonal, *cyclical,* or technological factors would not be "cured" invariably by wage reductions.[21] Leo Wolman was another of these labor economists who vigorously opposed wage cutting. As early as 1932 Wolman emphasized that wage cutting set in motion a decline in prices, through the reduction of labor costs. Cumulative deflation was of course a dangerous, uncontrollable procedure, in Wolman's view.

By 1932 W. B. Donham of Harvard's Graduate School of Business Administration was also concerned about wage cutting. Donham already had fears of secular stagnation, warning that U.S. experience might be similar to "the recent history of England and Germany, where for twenty or more years periods of prosperity have been disappointing both in duration and in the

21. Paul H. Douglas, *Real Wages in the United States* (Boston: Houghton Mifflin, 1930).

levels attained, and where unemployment is a permanent problem."[22] If we did nothing, Donham foresaw increasing unemployment and continued destruction of purchasing power. The Depression itself was sufficient evidence that reliance on "happy accidents" would be disastrous in the future. "The wonder is," Donham admitted, "that our haphazard economy has worked so well in the past."[23]

Increased demand and reduced unemployment were Donham's interests, and continuous work and high wages were essential to both. While wage cuts might be necessary in the microeconomic sense, Donham fully recognized that "every reduced pay envelope destroys the buying power of consumers."[24] In short, Donham endorsed all methods of increasing aggregate demand, such as public works, rebuilding the slum areas of large cities, etc. "We certainly shall be mad if, without trying anything but money and credit as a remedy, we supinely accept continuous unemployment," he concluded.[25]

Also in 1932 R. W. Stone, primarily a labor economist at the University of Chicago's School of Business Administration, commented that it was somewhat inevitable that maintenance versus reduction of wages should be a controversial issue. Stone argued, however, that a major factor in preventing considerable wage cutting in depression, particularly in the current one, "was the widely held conviction that cutting wages was economically unsound because of its effect on consumer purchasing power."[26] Here, then, is a case where pre-Keynesians, instead of being accused, as they are by a very large number of modern economists, of advocating wage reductions, are credited with preventing successfully what might have been even wider spread wage cutting.

Stone deplored the 1931 propaganda for wage cutting and the successive wage cuts imposed by many firms. This simply

22. Wallace B. Donham, "The Attack on Depressions," *Harvard Business Review*, 2 (October 1932), 47.
23. Ibid., p. 48.
24. Ibid., p. 54.
25. Ibid., p. 55.
26. R. W. Stone, "Wage Policies in Depression," *Journal of Business*, 5 (1932), 11.

was not the key to restoring normal employment. The way to restore full employment, Stone argued, is to increase investment. He explained that an expanding volume of investment would employ both idle human and property resources "and thereby provide the purchasing power necessary to absorb the increased volume of consumer goods that in the fullness of time would result from the new investment."[27]

This University of Chicago Professor of Economics relayed his message to Senator Wagner. In a 26 April 1932 letter to Senator Wagner, Stone argued that a public works program was indispensable to maintaining employment. Investment had to be expanded before significant recovery could occur, Stone contended, and since considerable private investment in the next half year was unlikely, it was all the more important that the federal government should develop such programs. Such a program, Stone said, could and should be financed by long-term bonds.

One of the most lucid refutations of wage cutting was E. H. Welch's in 1933. Connected both with the University of Pittsburgh and the Pennsylvania Department of Public Assistance, Welch explicitly pointed out, and thereby warned of the logical error of composition. "The problem of lowering wage rates in a particular industry or in a particular portion of an industry," Welch warned, "is entirely distinct from the problem of lowering general wage rates."[28]

Since 1929, Welch said, decreases in wholesale and retail prices had exceeded the decreases in wage rates, so that real wage rates had increased. Payrolls for this period, on the other hand, had decreased rapidly and unemployment had increased rapidly. This had led some to the conclusion that greater and more rapid wage cutting would have stimulated production and employment. What was their line of reasoning, he then asked. First, further reductions of general wage rates were presumed to result in a more rapid decline in costs, in turn resulting in one

27. Ibid., p. 26.
28. Emmett H. Welch, "The Relationship Between Wage Rates and Unemployment," *Journal of the American Statistical Association,* 28 (March 1933 Supplement), 54.

of two things. Either prices would decline still further or prospective profits would increase. "It is argued that the first possibility would have resulted in greater demand, and hence in greater employment," Welch said, "and that the second would have resulted in increased production and employment due to the profit incentive."[29]

This line of argument, Welch believed, should be evaluated, its tacit assumptions questioned. Would aggregate demand increase? Assume that employers reduced their unit selling prices by an amount commensurate with the reduction in unit costs, which was brought about by lower wage rates. If these reductions in wholesale prices were to augment demand, Welch continued, retailers would have to reduce their prices in order that the "savings" might be passed on to the consumers. This was unlikely, he argued, because "it is a well-known fact that retail prices do not fall nearly so soon nor nearly so much, either relatively or absolutely, as wholesale prices."[30]

Even if it were assumed that retail prices would decline commensurately with the rate of cost reduction, and he did not concede that this was likely, Welch did not see any assurance that aggregate demand would increase in proportion to the decrease in prices. This assumed price elasticity of demand for all goods, which was unrealistic. "Furthermore," he continued, "it is possible that more rapidly falling prices would have encouraged prospective purchasers to postpone their purchases still more than they have, hoping to buy at still lower price levels."[31] It was very doubtful, therefore, "whether reduced wage rates would have increased demand, and hence payrolls, by as large an amount as payrolls would have decreased by the reduction in wage rates."[32]

If wage reductions could not be relied upon to increase aggregate demand, could they be counted on to increase production? Assume that employers would not reduce their selling prices when wage rates were reduced. In order to place the argu-

29. Ibid.
30. Ibid., p. 55.
31. Ibid.
32. Ibid.

ment in its most favorable light, Welch said, further assume that lower wage rates did succeed in substantially increasing the prospects for profits, and hence production. Could the additional output be sold? There was no assurance that it could, Welch argued. The problem was not how to increase production but "how to distribute enough consumer's purchasing power to consume the goods we have produced and are able to produce."[33] Welch concluded that if an insufficiency of consumer's purchasing power was a factor crucial to the occurrence of a depression, any policy that tended to decrease consumers' purchasing power and hence consumption surely would not contribute to recovery.

A full two years later Otto Nathan at New York University was arguing for the maintenance of wage rates, although he too acknowledged that, in many microeconomic cases, such a policy might be impossible. He, too, presumed consumption to be a function of income, commenting that the "less payrolls are reduced, the more it will be possible to uphold consumption, to prevent the slump from spreading too much to the consumption goods industries, and to keep up a maximum of the 'normal' amount of goods exchanged."[34]

The professional literature of the period hardly suggests that the classical school, in point of fact, was populated by inveterate disciples of wage cutting at the first sign of unemployment. It does not even appear that the aforementioned economists were content to leave wages alone. Rather, they commonly warned against reduction of wages as a policy with harmful effects among which was a decrease in consumption spending.

PANACEAS

Although most of the professionally endorsed solutions to unemployment and deflation were more or less orthodox, some professional economists endorsed (and sometimes spawned for

33. Ibid., pp. 55–56.
34. Otto Nathan, "The N.I.R.A. and Stabilization," *American Economic Review*, 25 (March 1935), 48.

the benefit of amateurs) relatively bizarre and often complex means of recovery, viz., supplementary money schemes, anti-hoarding schemes, auxiliary economy schemes, new monetary standards, and so on. Some who helped organize "unemployed co-ops," however, did so to keep the members from starving, to assist them in making clothes for their children, to offer various forms of emergency assistance, in other words, but unmistakably not to carry the whole load of macroeconomic recovery. Food is the recognized panacea for hunger!

During the early 1930s the number of national "self-help" projects increased markedly. One variety involved a bold proposal for an outright separate economic system for the unemployed. In March 1932 the well-known Frank D. Graham (Princeton University) became perhaps the first important proponent of this policy of economic apartheid. He privately circulated a proposal calling for an Emergency Employment Corporation, a system designed to employ idle workers in producing commodities for their own consumption in a separate economy which utilized scrip redeemable only in goods produced within their system. The EEC was to be empowered with authority to enter into contractual agreements with existing producers for the production of consumers' goods. The contracting firms would be supplied with "consumption certificates," which would serve as their means of paying the labor costs involved in producing the incremental output.[35]

In terms of practical application, Graham proposed that contracts could be let among large mail order houses and staples' manufacturers which were producing at less than full capacity. The mail order houses would agree to increase their orders if the partially idle manufacturers would accept credits on the mail order house as a percentage of payment. The manufacturers would in turn use the credits to partially pay the wages of their workers. The workers, whose employment would increase as

35. Each week the EEC would calculate the redeemable value of each consumption certificate. Apparently, the EEC would estimate the total dollar value of weekly production and divide the total by the units of consumption certificates paid out during the week. Cf. Frank D. Graham, *The Abolition of Unemployment* (Princeton: Princeton University Press, 1932), pp. 14–29.

orders increased, would then redeem their wage-credits by "purchasing" the goods from the mail order houses.[36]

By 1934 a more ambitious plan had been drafted by University of Oklahoma Professors John B. Cheadle, Howard D. Eaton, and Cortez A. M. Ewing. Circulated widely by Eaton, their plan called for the establishment of an Industrial Stabilization Corporation. The ISC would contract for the production of goods with manufacturers who were willing to accept ISC notes. A limited form of nonlegal tender, the notes were to be obtained from the Federal Reserve by tender of the contractor. Contracting manufacturers would in turn use the notes to pay the wages of their employees who would redeem them in commodities sold in ISC stores. Their scheme also had an anti-hoarding device in the form of a discretionary monthly 0.5 per cent stamp requirement.[37]

Princeton's J. Douglas Brown, who was a former member of the President's Emergency Committee for Employment, managed to marshall an amazing amount of professional support for still another version of the barter-scrip movement. Brown circulated a petition which proposed federal and state aid for establishing a network of barter systems. Functioning outside of the normal market economy, the unemployed would produce for their own consumption.

Brown's particular brand of an auxiliary economy is most notable because of the stature and prestige of the petition signers, among whom the most prominent were Willard E. Atkins (New York University), Frank Aydelotte (President, Swarthmore College), C. Canby Balderston (University of Pennsylvania), George E. Barnett (Johns Hopkins University and President of the AEA), John Bates Clark (Columbia University and past President of the AEA), Joanna C. Colcord (Russell Sage

---

36. Ibid., pp. 91–99. In February 1933 W. I. King proposed a version of Graham's plan to the Senate Finance Committee. It is perhaps noteworthy that, among the various auxiliary economy proposals, only the Graham and King versions asserted that their plans would stimulate credit expansion. Other adherents, mostly the amateurs, backed the auxiliary economies on the notion that they directly employed idle workers.
37. John B. Cheadle, Howard O. Eaton, and Cortez A. M. Ewing, *No More Unemployment* (Norman, Okla.: University of Oklahoma Press, 1934), pp. 23–29, 105–19.

Foundation), Morris A. Copeland (University of Michigan and later President of the AEA), Paul H. Douglas (University of Chicago and later President of the AEA), Howard O. Eaton (University of Oklahoma), Frank Albert Fetter (Princeton University and past President of the AEA), Frank Whitson Fetter (Princeton University), Irving Fisher (Yale University and past President of the AEA), Walton H. Hamilton (Yale University), Paul V. Kellogg (Editor of *Survey Graphic*), Willford I. King (New York University), William M. Leiserson (Antioch College), Richard A. Lester (Princeton University), Harvey Leist Lutz (Princeton University), James D. Magee (New York University), Broadus Mitchell (Johns Hopkins University), Sumner H. Slichter (Harvard University and later President of the AEA), Charles T. Tippetts (University of Buffalo), Jacob Viner (University of Chicago and later President of the AEA), Charles R. Whittlesey (Princeton University), Joseph H. Willits (Dean of the University of Pennsylvania Wharton School), and Leo Wolman (Columbia University).

Most of these self-help movements appear to have been spontaneous reactions to a federal government which had failed to provide any real relief. The schemes were largely considered as emergency measures. No one apparently saw in them a permanent reform.

SOME ANTAGONISTIC CONTRACTIONISTS

More often than not, when contraction appeared to win the support of leading economists it did so by default. Pessimistic about government's proficiency in dealing with economic disaster and criticial of the results of its past attempts, these economists objected to proposals for increasing the public debt. James W. Angell of Columbia, for example, was a sometimes opponent of deficit spending primarily because it had not been effective in the past. He was not so much a contractionist, however. Angell pointed out that roughly two-thirds of the debt issued since 1930 had been created by the banking system. Although he felt this was a dangerous practice in terms of the future, Angell thought that a case could be made "for the view that, to date, this deposit inflation has been a good thing: that it has merely offset and prevented the further drastic contraction of total deposits which would otherwise have taken place, and that it has therefore really not been inflation after all."[38]

Angell then took to task four principal arguments which defenders of deficit spending commonly advanced. First, he did not accept altogether the argument that a national emergency existed, or that governmental borrowing was the only realistic way of raising enough money, or that if savings were inadequate to float the loans, currency or deposits had to be created for the purpose. Second, he admitted that government credit had to be extended to prevent the collapse of business enterprises, the loss of farms and homes, etc., but he countered that the crisis phase of the depression seemed well past, and these considerations could not be advanced to justify *further* large increases in the public debt.

A third defense of increases in public spending, Angell said, "is the familiar proposition that 'government spending stimulates business recovery.' "[39] (Witness that in this *1935* article, Angell claims that the proposition is a *familiar* one.) Angell did not so much disagree with this argument as specify the conditions which were necessary for it to hold. His replies sound very much like the modern objections to the balanced budget multiplier. Angell argued, first of all, that government spending must not displace private spending. To the extent that it did, the stimulus of public spending was nullified. Furthermore, additional governmental spending is effective in improving general economic conditions only as long as the governmental spending itself is continued. Even this "contractionist" seems to have been a harbinger to the "secular Keynes." Angell continued that the public spending must not discourage the revival of private business activity. Finally, Angell thought that Keynes and others exaggerated the multiplier.

The last argument for increased public spending affirmed

38. James W. Angell, "The Federal Finances and the Banking System," *Journal of the American Statistical Association, 30* (March 1935), 171.
39. Ibid., p. 172.

that "mild inflation is a good thing." Angell feared, however, that it would result in excessive inflation in the future. In recognition of a sort of "liquidity trap," as Keynes was to call it later, Angell argued that recovery appeared to demand "a revival of velocity, not an increase in quantity [of money]."[40]

Harvard's Leonard P. Ayres better fitted the caricature of the contractionist. He was opposed to deficit spending and to governmental attempts to restore prosperity in general. Relief expenditures were no help, he argued, because recipients spent the money on consumer goods, while it was in the durable goods industries that the unemployment problem was most severe. Most of the other emergency expenditures had gone for public works, which were an effective but costly means for providing employment, Ayres complained. Ayres apparently thought that construction costs would be driven up by public works expenditures, which tended to discourage private construction work.

What we needed most was not greater public appropriations, Ayres argued, but a removal of the obstacles to business recovery, e.g., regulations on business, fear about the future of money, and new regulations on security issues. If these obstacles only were removed, Ayres claimed, "we should then rapidly finance the recovery with private profit-making funds."[41]

C. J. Bullock was no more a contractionist than his Harvard colleague, Ayres, but he was a far more determined and outspoken one. Bullock frankly was opposed to the use of expansionary monetary and fiscal policy. "Priming the pump," Bullock charged, "had failed to start a natural flow of water through the pump," and it had paid little attention to the "destructive effects of public money upon the values of the pump, the condition of which depends upon public confidence and the spirit of enterprise."[42] Confidence and enterprise, apparently the keys to recovery, "would be immensely strengthened by the appearance of signs of natural recovery from terrible depression, but very cer-

40. Ibid., p. 174.
41. Leonard P. Ayres, "Problems of Recovery," *Journal of the American Statistical Association*, 30 (March 1935), 149.
42. C. J. Bullock. "Inflation by Public Expenditure," *Review of Economics and Statistics*, 16 (October 1934), 213.

tainly injured when such things as improvement in retail trade or increase in industrial activity are either suspected, or definitely known, to be due, at least in part, to the outpouring of funds from the Federal Treasury."[43]

Two months later Bullock continued to condemn mounting expenditures, an unbalanced budget, and other measures. "Raising rates of wages, at a time when millions of people were unemployed because employers could not hope to avoid loss if they increased their scale of operations, has proved to be a bad method of increasing employment."[44] Referring to the abandonment of a minimum wage by the Relief Administration and attempts to promote private construction by the Housing Administration, Bullock commented that these were encouraging signs. If this trend continued, if "destructive legislative measures" were avoided, and if steps could be taken toward balancing the federal budget, then greater improvements in economic conditions were foreseen by Bullock.

Another two months later Bullock began to complain about the federal budget in particular. He bitterly argued that public credit was strained dangerously and that this imprudent financial plan posed an obstacle in the path of recovery. He went on to attack social security legislation ("such measures are later broadened in scope, . . . the original benefits seldom satisfy the beneficiaries, . . . expenditures generally exceed all estimates."), the wage policy of the NRA ("the cost of labor . . . was already so high as to be an important contributing factor to general unemployment"), work relief projects ("the prospect of industrial recovery is less bright than it might have been if less ambitious and more economical methods of relief had been proposed and a substantial step had been taken toward reducing the expenditures which throw the budget so greatly out of balance.").[45]

W. L. Crum was another of the antiexpansionists, less adamant, however, than Ayres or Bullock. Crum favored a main

43. Ibid.
44. C. J. Bullock, "Reform vs. Recovery," *Review of Economics and Statistics,* 16 (December 1934), 263.
45. C. J. Bullock, "Reform, Recovery, and the Budget," *Review of Economics and Statistics,* 17 (February 1935), 49–52.

reliance upon "natural forces," but not an entire reliance upon them. Like his Harvard colleagues, he saw the key to recovery in business confidence.[46]

In brief, even the contractionists, or more properly perhaps, the antiexpansionists, do not seem to fit the classical mold exactly. Although a search of professional literature does turn up some economists who were opposed to expansionary policies, a search for pre-Keynesian wage cutters is a disappointing one. Most of the discussion of wage policy, as a matter of fact, seems to have consisted in arguments against reductions—private or public—of wages. As it has already been suggested, most of the leading economists appear to have favored expansionary policies, but some of them abandoned all professional inhibitions and supported some remarkably unorthodox panaceas.

46. W. L. Crum, "Official Policies and Economic Prospects," *Review of Economics and Statistics,* 16 (August 1934), 168–71.

The 1931–1932 Harris Foundation Meetings

⚉ IT IS ALWAYS DIFFICULT to bring together the leaders of any discipline for a direct confrontation of their respective ideas. Logistics alone often poses insurmountable problems. In both 1931 and 1932, however, enough of such problems were overcome that many of America's leading economists met in Chicago. The occasion in each year was the Norman Wait Harris Memorial Foundation Lectures and Round Tables.

1931 Meeting

The Eighth Institute of the Foundation, held from June 23 to July 2, 1931, is particularly noteworthy. In the first place, John Maynard Keynes was a visiting lecturer and active participant in the round table discussions. Second, the subject of the lectures and round table discussions was "Unemployment As A World Problem," and "classical" economists delivered papers on policy matters which revealed the tone of their professional opinion during this period. (See Appendix B for a list of those attending and participating in the 1931 round tables.)

"IS WAGE CUTTING THE WAY OUT?"

On 26 June 1931 the Harris Foundation turned its attention to the question, "Are wage cuts a remedy for unemployment?"[1]

1. Norman Wait Harris Memorial Foundation, *Reports of Round Tables: Unemployment as a World Problem* (Chicago: 1931), pp. 190–223. Location of further material cited from this source is indicated by page numbers in parentheses following the material.

In a joint effort, Professors Henry Schultz (University of Chicago) and Carter Goodrich (Columbia University) both treated the question at length and led subsequent discussion. Principally because of Keynes's presence, their treatment of wage policy is significant. It is moreover significant as a historical test of the caricature of "classical" economists.

Described as "a hard-boiled classicist," Henry Schultz opened the Friday afternoon session with a discussion of the foundations, interests and limitations of modern economic theory. Almost as if he suspected that one of his listeners, Keynes, would in only five years argue to the contrary, Schultz suggested that modern economic theory certainly rested on a much sounder logical as well as empirical basis than the economic theory of a century ago. According to Schultz, it was "a far cry between the economic theory of Ricardo's day and our own." (p. 192)

For example, Schultz pointed out that modern economists recognized the interrelationships of economic phenomena and that they cautiously used terms such as "the supply curve of labor." Particularly in the case of labor, Schultz continued, the long run was likely to be very long, if not to say too long. Labor questions simply required significant modifications in ordinary demand and supply analysis.

Schultz also admitted that "in spite of the fact that modern theory constitute[d] a great improvement over the classical theory," even the best of present theories was neither "designed to deal with" nor "meant to throw much light on cyclical fluctuations." (pp. 193–94) In Schultz's view, the remedy to the problem of depression consisted in bringing about a better relationship between cost and price. The alternative strategies were either a price policy approach, i.e., attacking the problem from the demand side, or a cost policy approach, i.e., working from the supply side. He apparently viewed wage, monetary, and fiscal policies as potential means of influencing cost-price relationships. Schultz's assignment, as he understood it, was that of considering the second possibility, viz., decreasing costs through wage cutting. Because he felt that there was no general dynamic theory of economics which embraced the theory of business cycles, Schultz argued that no general answer could be given the question, "Is wage cutting the way out?" The question had to be broken up, subdivided into several minor problems.

From the freely competitive, microeconomic point of view, Schultz immediately saw problems. Assuming that wages were cut and that they represented a significant proportion of the costs of production, a competitive firm might succeed in regaining a profit residual. If enough other firms were similarly successful in reducing their costs, it would appear that "the wheels of industry" would be started sufficiently. Schultz made it clear, however, that nothing in the competitive (diagrammatical) model suggested the *ultimate* effects of this policy. As a matter of fact, he regarded the assumption of free competition invalid for modern large-scale industry.

Schultz noted that the present depression was characterized by an unusual frequency of firms for which marginal costs exceeded price. How could a better relationship between price and cost be achieved? If wages were reduced, the marginal cost curves would be reduced accordingly, which in turn would appear to involve an increase in production. In order to know the ultimate effect of wage policy, Schultz kept emphasizing that "we have also to know the elasticity of demand of the commodity in question, and the relation between the elasticity of demand and the total market output." (p. 197) Schultz's point, therefore, was that the ultimate effect of wage policy must be assessed in terms of the effect on aggregate demand! Cost policy in general, and wage policy in particular, depended on the demand side for its ultimate effect—if cutting wages increased total demand, the ultimate effects were favorable; if they decreased demand, the ultimate effects were unfavorable.

Henry Schultz then relied upon Carter Goodrich, described as "a soft-boiled classicist," to analyze more carefully the conditions under which the ultimate effects of wage policy were favorable and unfavorable. If other prices fall, must the rate of wages fall? If there is widespread unemployment, must the rate of wages fall? As an extension of Schultz's discussion, Goodrich argued that neither of these questions could be given a single absolute answer, valid for all possible situations.

For purposes of distinguishing between the sorts of situations, Goodrich characterized four possible conditions which might affect industry. In each case he indicated the assumed length of time and extent to which industry would be affected by the particular condition: (1) prolonged falling prices due to technological improvement, long duration, general extent; (2) prolonged falling prices due to monetary causes, long duration, general extent; (3) prolonged depression in particular industries, long duration, partial extent; and (4) depression phase of business cycle, short duration, general extent. Was it possible to answer the question regarding wage reductions in each case?

Goodrich pointed out that the first case, falling prices due to technical improvement, had been discussed already by Professor Alvin H. Hansen (University of Minnesota), who had made it clear that there was no necessity for a general reduction in wages. Hansen had suggested that there was a long-run likelihood of an increase in real wages. He also suggested, however, that it was likely for technological improvement to lead to depressions in particular industries or groups of industries, in which wages might consequently fall. But in stimulated industries, wages were likely to be raised.

The second case, prolonged falling prices due to purely monetary causes, might lead to general reductions in nominal wages "due to the change in the value of the counters with which we are dealing." (p. 199) On the other hand, there was no reason for assuming either that this fall in wage rates would work out as a flat percentage reduction over the whole of industry or that the relative shares going to wages would remain constant.

Goodrich was not really concerned with the first two cases, since he considered cases three and four more relevant and urgent in the current situation. Regarding the third case, prolonged depressions of a single industry or single group of industries while the rest of industry is flourishing, Goodrich submitted that the argument for wage reduction in the depressed industries seemed very strong. Here, Goodrich was not suggesting a *policy* of wage reductions, but rather that wages should be *allowed* to fall. If wages were allowed to fall, they would simply perform their traditional function of directing labor out of what appears to be, over a long period, an unprofitable use. Of the four cases, Goodrich argued, this was the only one "in which a reduction in wages may have any value as a signal to move somewhere else, because in each of the other three cases the depression assumed, or the fall in prices assumed, is common to all industries, though of course varying in extent between different ones." (p. 200)

Finally, Goodrich came to case four, the depression phase of the cycle, which was most relevant to prevailing conditions. At last, here was an opportunity for the "classical" economists—not only Schultz and Goodrich but the other participants as well—to present the case for wage cuts as a remedy for unemployment and depression! Suppose, Goodrich suggested, that those presently employed have their wages cut by ten per cent. What would be the effects? The first effect, Goodrich submitted, was a ten per cent reduction of the incomes of employed workers, which in turn reduced aggregate demand! In Goodrich's words, "The first effect, or one of the first effects, at least, is to reduce by that ten per cent the purchasing power of those particular workers who are now employed, leading therefore to a reduction in the demand for workmen's commodities, at least, and therefore, probably to a reduction in the total demand for consumers' goods as compared to the total demand for producers' goods." (p. 201)

Goodrich admitted that some economists assumed such a wage reduction would have almost simultaneously still another effect upon employment and workers' incomes. They maintained that by reducing the cost of labor, business enterprises would be able to hire more labor at the lower wage rates and perhaps pay out more rather than less in total wages. Would this occur simultaneously? Would it occur at all? Goodrich doubted it. For one thing, he remarked, employers might see no market for any more output. "It may enable him to keep on going as he was," Goodrich pointed out, "but he will see no larger market at any price." (p. 201)

In short, Schultz and Goodrich reached the conclusion that "wage cutting is certainly no general panacea." (p. 206) Almost as if he suspected that Keynes would soon accuse all of his predecessors of committing a logical error of composition, Goodrich explicitly pointed out in conclusion that, in some cases, wage cutting "may be dubious in its effects on business in general, even when it is highly advisable from the point of view of the individual business." (p. 206) Rounding out this conclusion, Goodrich advanced two provocative points:

[F]irst, the great importance of the diagnosis of the situation that we are in. What *are* we in? I think Mr. [Sumner H.] Slichter raised the question the other night. Certainly in "4," but how much of "1" and "2" are relevant, and which industries, which parts of industries, and perhaps which countries, are in state "3"? Here our thinking is perhaps helped most by Dr. [Karl] Pribram's insistence that different countries and industries, even in this world-wide depression, are in very different situations, and where they are in the same trouble they are in that trouble for very different combinations of reasons. The second point I suggest is the importance of careful attention to the time factor. How long-run an effect are you working for? (pp. 206–7)

Schultz and Goodrich having completed their treatment of wage cutting, Chairman Quincy Wright announced that the subject was open for discussion by either the hard-boiled or the soft-boiled. Without identifying himself as one or the other, Professor Alvin Hansen spoke first from the floor and declared that he was "in general agreement with what Mr. Goodrich has said." (p. 207) A moment later, Sumner Slichter also agreed with Schultz and Goodrich, arguing that the question of whether wages should be maintained or cut was a meaningless one. The important thing, he argued, was to avoid further deflation, "and one can get further deflation, depending upon circumstances, either by cutting wages or by maintaining them." (p. 210)

A statement highly significant in light of his assault on the "classics" a short five years later, then followed—John Maynard Keynes gave his reactions to the Schultz and Goodrich analysis of wage cutting.

I think that this analysis which Mr. Schultz and Mr. Goodrich have given us is extraordinarily good and most helpful. I have never seen it put quite so before. This diversion seems to be vital in the discussion of this. I have very little to add to the actual scope of this, or to criticize. . . . (p. 212)

Keynes did want to add some thoughts on case four which defined, according to general agreement, the category in which the Depression most nearly belonged. The analysis he added, however, was not his own. "[I]t is due to a young English economist, Mr. R. F. Kahn," he explained. (p. 212) In the short run, to which case four belonged, Keynes assumed that employers would continue to produce so long as gross receipts exceeded prime, i.e., variable, costs. Keynes argued that the difference between total entrepreneurial receipts and output was related to the disparity between savings and investment. This is remarkably similar to the Clark and Douglas arguments that the difference between spending and income was related to the disparity. Keynes concluded that "the only way of increasing prime profit [the difference between gross receipts and total variable costs] is to increase the value of investment relatively to the amount of money saving." (p. 212)

Keynes suggested that this framework could be used to test whether or not a wage cut would increase employment. If wage cuts diminished the excess of saving, that is, the reduction would increase prime profit and enable manufacturers to increase production. But Keynes then proposed taking the case where the employer passed on the wage reduction in the form of lower prices. Since wages were not the whole of cost, a ten per cent reduction in wages would cause a less than ten per cent reduction in price, even if the whole of the wage cut were passed on. Consequently, there would be a simple transfer of purchasing power from the wage earner to the rentier class. Assuming that the rentier "probably" saves more than the wage earner, Keynes argued in this case that wage reductions would diminish prime profit and employment.

In Keynes's framework, therefore, the effect of wage reductions was a function of whether the increase of saving "would be greater or less than the increased amount of investment which might take place by the employers interpreting it, whether rightly or wrongly, as something in their favor." (pp. 212–15) Continuing, Keynes thought that a favorable influence, i.e., increase in the excess of investment over saving, became less likely as "overcapacity" spread in every direction. "[A]t the beginning of the slump," Keynes submitted, "there might be more to be hoped for from wage cuts than later in the slump." (pp. 212–15) In complete agreement with the "classical" economists, Keynes admitted openly that the net result of wage cuts "depends upon quantities which we are not in a position to measure," and that "there is a great deal which is indeterminate on both sides." (pp. 215–16)

Schultz, Goodrich, and Keynes then engaged in a discourse which indicated complete agreement among the three. Schultz, as a matter of fact, demonstrated that Keynes merely was repeating the "hard-boiled classical" analysis. Keynes agreed that if Schultz's "Cournot-Amoroso" formula were aggregated as Schultz suggested, "you get a formula by which you can relate the excess of saving to the volume of investment." (pp. 217–18) Keynes's agreement was in response to Schultz's conclusion that "the two analyses [Schultz's and Keynes's] are practically the same." (pp. 217–18)

In a subsequent discussion with Sumner Slichter, Keynes further demonstrated his affinity to the "hard-boiled classical" approach. He, too, wanted to know the elasticity conditions before advising on wage policy. When Slichter asked Keynes directly if he would favor a cut in wages in the construction industry, Keynes replied, "Whether it might help depends on whether the demand for housing were very elastic." (p. 222)

Just before the session on wage cuts ended, Schultz and Keynes exchanged commentaries on the state of European economics. These statements clearly imply that both men found significant differences in the theoretical framework of European and American economists, and thereby tend to discredit the subsequent classification of these two distinct groups under the single head, "classical."

MR. SCHULTZ: I think I can answer [the] question as to why so many European economists take the extreme view. My impression is that they are all influenced by Schumpeter, and he accepts the old marginal theory hook, bait, and sinker.

MR. KEYNES: I should add that Professor [A.C.] Pigou holds the theory just as you described. He says it is a perfectly simple story that there is a one-to-one relation between the volume of employment and the level of real wages. (p. 223)

If one expected a fight staged between "hard-boiled classicists" (who would be cutting every wage in sight) and a "sentimental laborite" (who would be echoing John L. Lewis's slogan of "no backward step"), he must be disappointed at the faint evidence of combat which appears. As a matter of fact, Goodrich revealed that many had expected such a battle to develop between Schultz and himself, but he felt that such expectations were foolish. At any rate, this 1931 discussion of wage rates and unemployment is historically significant evidence that the leading economists in the *United States* were unconvinced that wage cutting, or even allowing wages to fall, would augment employment, production, income, or any other relevant aggregate. The 1931 confrontation between Keynes and this group of economists—often—indiscriminately designated merely as "classical"— far from revealing a polarization of views, testifies more nearly to a consensus.

The congruity of their approaches, analyses, formulations regarding depression appears strikingly in the responses to Schultz's and Goodrich's emphasis on the ultimate or the aggregate effects of wage policy. In their argument, they specified that wage reductions were favorable to recovery *only* if they augmented aggregate demand. Also, Goodrich explicitly warned against the logical error of composition in the case of wage policy. In response to these views, Keynes and the other economists acknowledged their agreement. It is cases such as this, especially when coupled with Keynes's Foreword to the German edition of the *General Theory*, that lead easily to the conclusion that Keynes never intended to include leading American economists within the purview of the "classical economists" against whom he directed his assault.

THE ROLE OF GOVERNMENT AND OF INDIVIDUAL MANAGEMENT IN PREVENTING AND REMEDYING UNEMPLOYMENT

On June 29 Professor Joseph Willits (University of Pennsylvania) and Isador Lubin (Brookings Institution) delivered papers on the roles governmental and individual management might play in the prevention and remedy of unemployment.

Professor Willits, who spoke first, spared very few moments before launching his thesis. Reliance on individual action would
retard recovery, he argued. "If we are going to depend, as a
great many people in important places feel we must depend,
upon efforts by individual management to attack the problem
in the next ten years," Willits predicted, "when 1938 or 1939
roll around, I think we won't be much better prepared for dealing with a depression than we are now." (p. 229)

Willits went further to actually blame laissez-faire for the
economy's plight. The remedies, therefore, lay in more control,
not less. The inevitability of an increasing public role was
clearly forecast, according to Willits, by the trend visible in the
recommendations of the 1931 participants for dealing with unemployment. Consistent with the general trend of this policy
discussion, wage reductions simply were not mentioned by Willits
as a remedy for depression. But public works were.

Chairman Quincy Wright, noticing that the Willits and
Lubin papers had little to say for individual action, tried desperately to solicit the arguments of anyone who favored such
action. It seemed to Wright that the discussion "should be directed primarily to the broadest aspect of the problem between
government action and action by private individuals, namely,
the question of whether anything can be said for the policy of
individualism, which [Wright believed to be] advocated by the
distinguished citizen who occupies the White House, as against
policies that might be broadly described as socialistic." (p. 246)
Even when their recommendations were "broadly described as
socialistic," *not one* of the participants spoke for the individualistic position.

Again, Chairman Wright pleaded for someone to argue explicitly against government interference, or, even better, for
someone to sponsor the individualistic position. When no one
spoke accordingly, Wright commented on this remarkable consensus. "I do not know exactly what it means," Wright said
glumly, "that here in the middle of America we seem to have
so few advocates for an outright abandonment of this whole
problem by government, which seems to be our actual policy to
a large extent." (p. 263)

Throughout the session on the respective roles of government and individuals, the air was filled with charges that President Hoover was *not* following the advice of the profession. None of the economists felt able to advance a case for the individualistic position to which Hoover allegedly was wedded. It is, moreover, notable that, in a session devoted to the prevention of and remedy for unemployment, not one of these leading American economists even mentioned wage cutting. To the extent the economic policy of the Depression at this time embodied classical principles, it was not on the advice of these economists. Their views already stood in critical judgment of prevailing policies.

PUBLIC WORKS CONSTRUCTION AND UNEMPLOYMENT

On the evening following the discussion of public and private management during depression, Dr. Otto Nathan led a discussion of public works and unemployment. Nathan quickly pointed out that questions of public works and either business cycles or unemployment were only part of a still larger problem, viz., the problem of the interrelationship between public finances and business cycles. Sounding much like developers of the full employment budget, Nathan pointed out that "we do know . . . that the public finances are influenced very largely through business cycle movements; but on the other hand, public finances and the finances of all public authorities influence to a certain degree the business cycle fluctuations." (pp. 267–69)

Nathan argued for a "very conscious policy of revenue and expenditure of public authorities" with an eye toward making "the policy of public works a very considerable check to the business cycle movement." (pp. 267–69) Orders and spending were not all that would be augmented, Nathan felt. Much along pump-priming lines, he moreover felt that public works would give a "psychological incentive to the business people as a whole" or, stated alternatively, "a real incentive for the overcoming of this dead point." (pp. 271–72) Nathan, in short, was convinced that investment spending was the key to recovery but that bleak expectations had curtailed such spending. "[T]he very fact private people are not likely to use money available to them in banks," Nathan submitted, "the very fact that they are still too frightened to make new investments, must induce governments to do so on their own behalf, and must induce governments to do something to overcome the dead point business is in." (pp. 271–72)

Nathan's discussion was seriously limited and influenced by an initial assumption, based on historical grounds, that a countercyclical public works policy would be too small. Still, he advanced two related fiscal policies. First, he thought that it was an advisable financial policy for governments to float loans in times of depression for those public works which were going to be erected. Second, he endorsed the plan calling for governmental accumulation of financial reserves during prosperity and disposal of the reserves during depression.

The initial reaction to Nathan's discussion centered on his notion of waiting until the Depression had established a new equilibrium before executing the public works program, which was based on his assumption that government had smaller amounts of medicine than the curing of the ills required. I. Lubin and Keynes were particularly critical of this assumption. Lubin's point—it is notable that Keynes was silent on this—was that there could be more than one balance or equilibrium. Nathan readily agreed, but still he insisted that government must wait until one of the possible balances was established.

Interestingly enough, Alvin Hansen was the *only* participant who seemed to deny the possibility of more than one equilibrium, e.g., the possibility of any one of a number of underemployment equilibria. A Chicago economist—the "hard-boiled classicist," Henry Schultz—charged that in contrast to other economists, Hansen was bound by the unrealistic assumption of perfect competition:

Mr. HANSEN: You must have a balance which is in terms of the proper relation of the prices of the different agents of production to their relative efficiencies. There is not more than one balance there; there cannot be a hundred balances.

MR. SCHULTZ: [I]t is not true that there may not be more than one balance. What actually happens is that you have a range within which an indefinite number of balances, or rather, points of equilibrium, may take place. (p. 285)

After much discussion about when to execute public works and how much spending was necessary, the "classical" economists had the opportunity to listen to Keynes. Keynes rightly pointed out that Nathan's course unfortunately was based fundamentally on the assumption that the amount of ammunition the government has is very small. Need it be very little, Keynes asked. The test of "adequacy," Keynes argued, was related to the question of how far below normal private investment has fallen. If total construction in 1928 were $10 billion and fell to $7 billion in 1930, then $3 billion was the measure of how much was needed, Keynes argued. "I think it is correct," Keynes continued, "that historically these ideas were initiated by the Webbs in their minority report on unemployment." (p. 293) Keynes also made it clear that the money should be raised by borrowing and that the funds should be easily and sufficiently available.

MR. KEYNES: If the money is raised in the ordinary way on the market, the government is coming into the market, and is taking the place of it. . . . There is always exactly the right amount available. Going back to my illustrative figures, suppose $10,000,000,000 total investment represents normal in this country. Private investment drops to $7,000,-000,000. The government steps in for the $3,000,000,000. . . . The government never wants more than the actual difference, you see. (pp. 294–95)

Only moments later, however, Keynes watered down his recommendation considerably when he shifted his attention directly to the United States. He made it clear that the case for public works in the United States was "much weaker" than in England. He also emphasized that the task of getting back to "a state of equilibrium" (Keynes apparently did not agree with the suggestions that more than one equilibrium was possible) should rest with monetary policy and not fiscal policy. In Keynes's words:

I think the argument for public works in this country is much weaker than it is in Great Britain. In Great Britain I have for a long time past agitated very strongly for a public works program, and my argument has been that we are such a center of an international system that we cannot operate on the rate of interest, because if we tried to force the rate of interest down, there is too much lending, and we lose our gold. The advantage of a government program in Great Britain is that the government can borrow at whatever the world rate of interest is, regardless of whether the investment yields that.

In this country you haven't a problem of that kind. Here you can function as though you were a closed system, and I think all your argument hitherto has been rather based on the closed system assumption. For such a system I would use as my first method operating on the long term rate of interest. If I could not do that, I should be afraid we would be open to the difficulty you suggested.

I think in this country deliberate public works should be regarded much more as a tonic to change of business conditions, but the means of getting back to a state of equilibrium should be concentrated on the rate of interest. That condition not being so in Great Britain, one had to lay great stress on public programs but in this country I should operate on the rate of interest.[2]

Consistent with the other sessions, the meeting on public works was characterized by a remarkable accord. Most, if not all, of the economists present questioned neither the efficacy nor the advisability of public works as a remedy for unemployment and depression. Attention was directed instead only to questions concerning the timing and extent of a public works program. Keynes and Hansen were really the only ones to weaken the case for public works.

IS IT POSSIBLE FOR GOVERNMENTS AND CENTRAL BANKS TO DO
ANYTHING ON PURPOSE TO REMEDY UNEMPLOYMENT?

On July 1 John Maynard Keynes himself was scheduled to discuss governmental and central bank action regarding unemployment. Inasmuch as the other round tables had encroached upon part of his topic, Keynes concentrated on central bank

2. Ibid., p. 303. As did Myrdal (1939), Keynes expected too much of the interest rate.

action. Speaking only briefly, he left matters largely to subsequent discussion. Actually, Keynes already had familiarized the assemblage with his theories of the interest rate and of central banking. He had argued a few days earlier that an excessive interest rate was to blame for falling prices and that he preferred central bank action to cure such problems. Keynes said:

> My theory . . . is that when prices are falling it is because the rate of interest is too high. Although the rate of interest may be low, it is never falling fast enough, therefore prices fall too. When it is rising it never rises fast enough. There are always drags on it. The pace is never sufficient, consequently the movement of prices is exactly the opposite of what you might expect in almost any theory. . . .
>
> I should agree that the capitalistic society as we now run it is essentially unstable. The question in my mind is whether one could preserve the stability by the injection of a moderate degree of management; whether in practice it is beyond our power to do this, and that we will have to have some further plan of control. I should like to try the central bank method first, uncertain how far in practice it would lead us. (pp. 67, 93)

In the discussion which followed Keynes's paper, the University of Chicago's Lloyd Mints tried to get him to focus on fiscal policy rather than monetary policy regarding unemployment, deflation, and depression in general. Keynes admitted that he was counting on the *interest rate* to equilibrate saving and investment. Mints wanted Keynes to agree that *fiscal policy*, primarily through its influence on investment spending, was more reliable.

> Mr. Mints: I should like to revert for a moment to the question of the relative importance of lowering the interest rate and public works. As I understand your argument, you want to reduce the interest rate in order to bring about an equivalence between saving and investment. As a matter of fact, won't public works bring about precisely the same results, not through decreasing the rate of interest, but increasing the rate of return for business firms, thereby increasing the rate of investment, even at current rates of interest?

> Mr. Keynes: Certainly, therefore I am in favor of an admixture of public works. . . . I should use the public works program to fill in the

interregnum while I was getting the interest down. The public works program would in itself increase business profits, and therefore relieve people from that exceptional unwillingness to borrow.

I should be afraid of that as a sole remedy. I should be afraid it would work itself out, come to an end, and then we should be back where we were unless we decided on a very definite further action. (pp. 493–94)

Without exception, Keynes gave everyone the distinct impression that he regarded "central bank action as being on the whole rather more important than government action." (pp. 501–2) Keynes commented:

I attribute importance to government action in the short run, and to central bank action in the long run. If we were prepared for a degree of socialism which we are probably not prepared for, I should modify my action. Unless we are prepared to be much more socialistic than we have been hitherto, there is a definite limit to what governments can do. (pp. 501–2)

Keynes's paper and its subsequent discussion were rather uninspiring and disappointing. He persisted in arguing that monetary policy, particularly manipulation of the interest rate, was the key to recovery from depression. Until the interest rate could be reduced to a level consistent with equilibrium between saving and investment, Keynes was counting on fiscal policy as a transitional tonic. From these views the group of "classical" economists present dissented. They were convinced that investment spending would not be influenced even by the lowest interest rates imaginable, and that fiscal policy was the key to recovery, both in the transitional and the enduring sense.

WAGE CUT REVISITED

Following E. J. Phelan's (International Labor Office) paper on "International Mechanisms and Unemployment," wage policy was again discussed. Among other points, Phelan argued that there appeared to be no mechanism through which wage cuts could be executed. Henry Schultz, the "hard-boiled classicist," was first to agree solidly with Phelan. Even if a "body of international experts" agreed that a reduction of wages would be desirable, Schultz emphasized that he saw no possibility of implementing such recommendations. Thinking primarily of the United States, Schultz concluded that labor would not agree to wage reductions. Even if economists recommended wage reductions, no means of enforcement were available. This was true for "nominal" wages and more particularly for "real" wages. On Schultz's commentary concerning wage reductions, his fellow "classical" economists concurred.

Finally Sumner Slichter said what one suspects was felt by all of the participants. The question of wage reductions was a dead issue. In Slichter's words:

From the standpoint of the United States, . . . I wonder if the wage issue . . . isn't becoming pretty academic. The reaction which seems to occur is, "Well, if a wage cut is made, it means a cut in the President's salary, and a cut in the General Manager's salary." You can't have a salary cut at the same time. Men fight awfully hard before they will cut their salaries. I expect in ten years to see it a dead issue in this country. I think it is practically a dead issue in this depression. (pp. 544–55)

There was no disagreement with Slichter's conclusion.

Overview of 1931 Meetings

As a remedy for unemployment, or for that matter, as a remedy for anything, wage cutting was from all appearances a dead issue as early as 1931. An outline distributed by Schultz and Goodrich at the 1931 Harris Foundation meetings clearly demonstrates this point. In it, they contrasted the "traditional" solution and their own. The traditional answer to the quesion of wage policy and unemployment, they pointed out, consisted in the following line of reasoning: "if labor is unemployed, it is therefore overvalued; reduce its price, and more will be taken off the market." (p. 191)

The traditional solution for unemployment, Schultz and

Goodrich suggested, was intended for cases where changes in the wage rate were useful as "signals." It was not intended for cases involving the depression phase of business cycles. Here, changes in wage rates, viz., reductions, were useless as signals. Wage reductions moreover were ridden with perverse influences which impeded recovery. Most important among these perverse effects was the "first" one—"the decrease in demand for consumers' goods." (p. 191) Their conclusion? Wage rates were "not sacrosanct," but cutting them was "no panacea." (p. 191)

Notably, no economist was willing to sponsor individual action as opposed to government action. Public works were consistently supported as the only effective means of dealing with depression. Keynes believed that public works should function as a short-run deterrent until the interest rate brought saving and investment into line. The American economists, on the other hand, saw in public works a means for augmenting spending and for enhancing the rate of return on investment. So far had they evolved beyond the classical ideational framework by 1931 that these leading American economists appear then to have solidly supported expansionary fiscal policy.

Despite the approximate consensus among the participants of the 1931 Harris Foundation meetings, they did not choose to organize a committee with a mandate to draft a statement of policy recommendations. They were content instead to confront each other with their respective ideas and to leave policy persuasion to the personal judgment of each individual.

1932 Meeting

Only six months later, after meetings on gold and monetary stabilization, participants in the 1932 Harris Foundation discussions (see Appendix B) showed a rapidly growing discontent with official depression policy and, reversing their earlier decision, judged it necessary to use the prestige of the Institute in a policy effort. Many of the members (the most widely-known ones) participated accordingly in the drafting of "recommendations designed to arrest deflation and to restore business activity to a normal level.[3] Impatient with prevailing policy and eager to have the weight of professional opinion felt in Washington, the Institute's officers were authorized to transmit the recommendations via telegram to President Hoover.

WHAT SHOULD BE DONE IN THE PRESENT EMERGENCY

By early 1932 Irving Fisher (age 65) had become so concerned about depression conditions that he had already severed ties at Yale University and had begun devoting virtually full time to policy persuasion in the Washington area. In keeping with his new role as (self-styled) Washington's economist-in-residence, Fisher appeared at the 1932 Harris Foundation round tables to lead a discussion of "what should be done in the present emergency."

Fisher did not claim to have a complete theory of depressions, and he did not really think that any explanation could be complete. He did predict, on the other hand, that it would be recognized ultimately that there is truth in most theories. Fisher's own insight into the problem of depression was related to the consequences of "overindebtedness." Not attempting at all to explain how overindebtedness comes about in the first place, Fisher was more concerned with its consequences and remedies. By overindebtedness, Fisher apparently meant an *excess demand for money.*

The first consequence of overindebtedness, i.e., an excess demand for money, was a fall in prices caused presumably by the accompanying excess supply of commodities. Those who are "overburdened" with debt are trying to sell, and as the selling grows in volume, it becomes distress selling, driving prices still lower. Whereas we are attracted normally by a high price, Fisher suggested, overindebtedness causes selling to accelerate as prices fall. Fisher emphasized, however, that distress

3. Norman Wait Harris Memorial Foundation, *Reports of Round Tables: Gold and Monetary Stabilization* (Chicago: 1932), pp. 412–15. Location of further material cited from this source is indicated by page numbers in parentheses following the material.

selling would cause only a mild decrease in the price level. The major problem of a debt-motivated excess demand for money was "the contraction of the currency that goes with it, for when a debt is paid to a commercial bank, of course it wipes out that much circulating medium." (p. 198) While this contraction of "circulating medium" was offset in normal times by other people's going into debt, Fisher submitted that a state of debt-motivated excess demand for money causes a massive movement toward selling, a contraction of the currency, and a fall in the general level of prices.

Overindebtedness also would damage production, Fisher continued. Profits would suffer because receipts would fall more rapidly than costs could be reduced. There would be a corresponding contraction of production. With the contraction of production, Fisher argued, "you have the discharge of employees and increase of unemployment, and as a consequence of the bankruptcies and the unemployment and the losses there comes, of course, psychologically a state of pessimism and distress, a lack of confidence, and that starts up another vicious circle, one of the consequences of which is hoarding, first in the banks, because the distress leads to getting rid of risky securities and substituting cash, which is one thing people in fear of bankruptcy want." (p. 199) Fisher was disturbed particularly over the prospect that reductions in the *nominal* rate of interest might be offset by a countervailing force—deflation in the general price level of commodities. This factor would drive the *real* rate of interest far higher than the nominal, imposing an abnormally heavy burden on debtors. Fisher went so far as to assert, "When there is deflation, you can reduce the nominal rate of interest to zero and still have a real rate of interest of fifty per cent per annum." (pp. 199–200)

In short, then, Fisher was arguing that a debt-motivated excess demand for money depresses commodity prices, meaning that the very effort to reduce debts tended to increase them. The way to overcome a depression so caused, therefore, was to check and reverse the excess demand for money. As far as Fisher was concerned, therefore, the answer to depression was to raise the price level enough to cure overindebtedness and thereafter to stabilize the price level. The immediate problem, accordingly, involved raising the price level either by increasing the circulating medium or by increasing its velocity. Along this line, Fisher distributed a list of twenty-four ways to favorably influence the stock of money or its velocity, and he asked his colleagues to rank these measures according to their respective preferences. Fisher made it clear that he wanted to return to Washington equipped with a lengthy list of policy alternatives, variously endorsed by the profession, which could help convert policy makers to his persuasion.

One of the earliest reactions to Fisher's discussion, and one shared by most participants, was registered by Herbert Feis, a Department of State official. Feis was concerned that Fisher's list of twenty-four measures did not include any which would add immediately and directly to consumers' purchasing power. In other words, why not public works?

Fisher argued that public works had been ineffective and tended to undermine public confidence in other remedies. His "classical" audience simply would not sit still on this issue. Harold Moulton (Brookings Institution) delivered a lengthy rebuttal which embraced many points on which participants ultimately agreed. Moulton argued that Fisher's notion seemed to be based on the assumption that pumping money into the channels of circulation automatically would raise the price level. To the contrary, Moulton argued, open-market operations *failed* to get money into the channels of circulation except to a limited extent. The trouble was not that banks had no money to lend or that interest rates were not already low. "The trouble lies on the one hand in the risks involved in business," Moulton submitted, "and on the other hand, in the unwillingness of solvent borrowers to pay even two or one per cent under the conditions of uncertainty that now prevail." (pp. 224–28)

The only way that banks could get money into circulation was through lending processes, Moulton declared. He doubted, however, that interest rates as low as two per cent could stimulate the amount of borrowing. If putting money into circulation were needed, Moulton argued, it should be done *directly* through government credit. Credit or purchasing power should be acquired from the Federal Reserve banks through the sale of bonds, and the money should be spent for the relief of unemployment, public works, etc. The difference between expansionary monetary policy and expansionary fiscal policy, Moulton argued, was that deficit financing of public works actually piped money into circulation, money which is "spent in the market, [setting] up a chain of demand all the way back through the economic system." (pp. 224–28)

Jacob Viner agreed wholeheartedly with Moulton and criticized the poor way in which public works had been used in the past as a depression remedy. "What you probably need," Viner suggested, "is a means whereby the banks can take up the increased government indebtedness through a relaxation of eligibility rules and other things, and the funds getting to the consumers through public expenditures." (pp. 228–29) The trouble with public works programs in the past, Viner complained, was their failure to be "connected with any procedure for increasing the net amount of banking funds in use." (pp. 228–29)

Under insurmountable pressure from his "classical" colleagues, Fisher recanted and added public works to his list of monetary measures. Only Alvin Hansen seemed unconvinced of the efficacy of public works as a remedy. Hansen, who appears to have been the only economist in attendance who approximately fitted the classical mold, felt that public works were, among other things, wasteful. In Alvin Hansen's words:

I have a feeling that public works has been accepted around the Round Table rather too easily tonight. Isn't it true that in the history of Great Britain and Germany they have after all devoted a great deal of attention to the question of public works, and never found public works any sort of remedy for the situation. There are a good many arguments against public works as an emergency measure. . . . You can't put public works suddenly into motion without an enormous waste, and you have to pay for them eventually, and they do react upon the private economy. (pp. 244–45)

Viner delivered a rebuttal which apparently quieted Hansen's anxiety regarding public works, for Hansen did not say another word for the duration of the meetings. In the first place, Viner argued, the history of public works was virtually irrelevant to the present situation. Public works in the past had been trivial, and none was connected with a program of currency expansion. In the second place, Viner continued, public works would have an *altogether favorable* reaction on other business. Finally, Viner charged, "so far as wasting is concerned, assume that there was thirty, forty, or fifty per cent wastage, it would be thirty, forty, or fifty per cent of the wastage involved now in the idle capital resources and the idle labor resources that are available and not being used."[4] What a strange scene— one of the founders of a "school" which was "less enamored with Keynesian ideas" than the rest of the profession trying to persuade one who became the most enamored with Keynesian ideas to adopt what might easily be described in retrospect as a Keynesian idea!

Fisher's discussion was provocative. Policy oriented and recently devoted almost completely to the Washington scene, Fisher left no doubt about his intentions. He was going to return to Washington, remedies in hand, and claim the endorsements of his colleagues. This posed somewhat of a problem. On the one hand, they did not want their names linked to ineffective or radical proposals, but, on the other hand, they did not want to embarrass Fisher, one of the profession's elders. In an attempt to avoid either horn of what was potentially a dilemma, a group of leading economists decided that they should organize collectively and draft a statement of responsible recommendations which most of them would feel comfortable signing. Also, they decided that they would give Fisher credit for having inspired the group's meeting and include him on the committee.

RECOMMENDATIONS DESIGNED TO ARREST DEFLATION AND TO RESTORE BUSINESS ACTIVITY TO A NORMAL LEVEL

On 30 January 1932 a committee of six—Irving Fisher, Alvin H. Hansen, Charles O. Hardy, Henry Schultz, Jacob Viner, and John H. Williams—met and in fact drafted a statement of rec-

4. Ibid., p. 245. Cf. Appendix A, pp. 155–56 for copy of telegram.

ommendations. The following day, Chairman Wright announced
to the Institute that the committee's report was ready. Henry
Schultz read the committee's report and announced that there
would be a special session later in the day. They recommended
that (1) cover for Federal Reserve notes should be liberalized
to include both federal government securities and commercial
paper; (2) open-market operations should be pursued systematically both to facilitate government financing and to increase
bank liquidity; (3) the Reconstruction Finance Corporation
should make loans to banks on assets ineligible for rediscount
with Federal Reserve banks; (4) the federal government should
maintain its expenditures at a level not lower than that of
1930–31; (5) intergovernmental debts should be reduced or
cancelled; and (6) tariffs and other barriers to world trade should
be negotiated with other countries. (pp. 366–67)

An hour after Schultz's report, a special session of economists
attending the Institute was held.[5] Speaking for the committee,
Professor Viner confessed that there had been some differences
in opinion among economists, who were in "disrepute on the
ground that we can never agree with each other, partly on account of the fact that we are disagreeing about terminology, not
understanding each other's functions, or that we disagree on details and do not think it necessary to talk about the things obvious to all of us."[6] Even in drafting the recommendations,
Viner admitted, there were some differences of opinion, "and this
is a minimum program on which we could agree."[7]

As the Special Session progressed, there was still further
disagreement, albeit mild. G. Haberler was upset regarding the
second recommendation, which endorsed the double aim of open-
market operations. While he agreed that, in America, the role
of facilitating government financing was not a dangerous one
for open-market operations, the same was not necessarily true of
Europe, he argued. Viner countered that the federal government would be unable to finance its deficits without the coopera-

5. Minutes, 31 January 1932, Special Session of Economists in Attendance at
the Norman Wait Harris Institute.
6. Ibid., pp. 1–2.
7. Ibid., p. 2.

tion of banks. Virtually intransigent on the issue, Haberler insisted that the report should say merely "with the aim to increase the liquidity of the banking structure."[8] Henry Simons retorted, however, that the aim of "facilitating necessary government financing" was very important because, in his words, "there is nothing [else] in the report which urges against deflationary measures of public finance."[9] Actually, Simons was wrong, and Charles Hardy rightly reminded him that, in the fourth recommendation, a budget deficit was required to maintain government services at the level of 1931.

Despite a lengthy discussion by the Special Session, the committee's report remained essentially unchanged. Twenty-four of the Institute's best-known participants agreed to sign their names to a telegram to President Hoover urging him to act favorably on each of them. (See Appendix A, p. 156.) Their recommendations received wide attention and occasional credit for persuading the Hoover administration to adopt its meager inflationary measures: (1) what later became the Glass-Steagall Act; (2) open-market purchases; (3) RFC aid to banks with ineligible assets; (4) public works programs financed by deficits; and (5) federal unemployment relief.

Overview of 1932 Meetings

The 1932 Harris Foundation is still another demonstration that the leaders of the economics profession were *not* recommending wage cuts as the solution to the Depression. Wage policy simply was never mentioned, despite the fact that the highlight of the entire meetings was the drafting of recommendations. The sympathy of these leaders of the profession was clearly and strongly along lines of monetary and fiscal expansion. As a matter of fact, the *minimum* program on which there was substantial agreement was *strongly* expansionist. Individually, there was in most cases an even stronger expansionist persuasion. ✿

8. Ibid., pp. 11–12.
9. Ibid., p. 12.

6

A Note on Commission Reports

■■ AS 1932 drew to a close, economists and other social scientists grew increasingly impatient with policy makers. Many acknowledged leaders of the profession agreed that commissions of inquiry should be formed. In this way, economists could remain nonpartisan, and at the same time, add to the prestige and persuasive power of their efforts. Generally motivating this decision was their awareness that the country desperately needed a unified national policy. So, the rare combination of basic dissatisfaction with prevailing methods of treating depression problems and a sense of the country's need for their services led social scientists to form several authorized commissions in late 1932 to study, analyze, and prescribe. Two of these commission reports stood above the others because of the prestige of their official members and the attention they received in official and professional surroundings. These were the equally famous reports on *Economic Reconstruction* by the Columbia University Commission[1] and *International Economic Relations* by the Commission of Inquiry into National Policy in International Economic Relations.[2]

1. *Economic Reconstruction: Report of the Columbia University Commission* (New York: Columbia University Press, 1934).
2. *International Economic Relations: Report of the Commission of Inquiry into National Policy in International Economic Relations* (Minneapolis: University of Minnesota Press, 1934).

Economic Reconstruction

In his Annual Report for 1932 Columbia President Nicholas Murray Butler cited problems which urgently needed the highest level of intelligent study. He called accordingly both for rigorous analysis and for constructive formulation of policy, in regard to the social and economic problems of the times. On 28 December 1932, therefore, he commissioned a group which included "various members of the Columbia University staff, some leading economists from other universities and also some students . . . whose work lay outside the academic field."[3] Including names such as Berle, Clark, Hansen, Mitchell, Schumpeter, and Viner, this was truly a blue-ribbon commission. (See Appendix A, p. 159.)

The General Report of the Columbia Commission was transmitted to President Butler on 31 January 1934. Right away, the Commission made it clear that three particular groups of problems faced them: "(1) problems of immediate recovery measures; (2) problems of long-range measures for the control of industrial fluctuations in the future; (3) problems of policies for the tapping of unused productive powers in good times (a) by increasing effective demand, (b) by raising the productiveness of backward producers nearer to the standards of the best, (c) by raising the standard of the best." (p. 11)

The key to understanding the Report lies in noticing the attention which the Commission devoted to augmenting *aggregate demand* as the essential requisite for recovery (cf. the third problem above). Undoubtedly, this insight can be traced largely to J. M. Clark, whose Special Report for the Commission indicated that chronic limitations of production were caused by limitations of effective, i.e., aggregate, demand. (p. 105–26) Clark actually focused on means whereby potential production capacity could be converted into realized production, "balanced and activated by an equivalent effective demand for the products turned out." (p. 105) In his Special Report, he also noted that the in-

3. *Economic Reconstruction*, p. v. Location of further material cited from this source is indicated by page numbers in parentheses following the material.

creased power to produce goods was impeded by the "tendency toward saving a progressively increasing proportion of our income as our income itself gets larger." (p. 109)

The General Report was clearly in the camp of the "reflationists." They argued that the primary immediate need, insofar as the monetary system was concerned, was "a rising price level reflecting an increased volume of business and increased employment, and associated with general confidence in the price-raising methods or impulses." (p. 33) In regard to this immediate desideratum, the General Report suggested that there were two methods of deliberately seeking a higher price level, emphasizing that both methods depended on governmental action.

The *direct* method of raising the price level operated on the monetary system. In its most drastic forms, this method amounted to a depreciation of the currency by "creating new money *ad hoc,* devaluating the dollar to a fixed quota of its former gold content, establishing a new and broader metallic basis for the issuance of currency, increasing the price of gold by governmental purchases, and so forth." (p. 34) On the other hand, less drastic forms of the direct method could be used, such as "increasing the supply of money, through the banks, provided the country is no longer subject to the controls of the gold standard, by means of a low Federal Reserve rediscount rate supported by security purchases on a lavish scale, thus supplying member banks with cheap money." (p. 34)

Regardless of the form of the direct method taken to raise the price level, however, it was seriously limited. The direct method could be successful, the Commission submitted, only if it could increase the *demand* for credit as well as the *supply* of it. Making borrowing easy or money cheap, in other words, could not guarantee a recovery of business activity. "Unless effective measures are found to increase purchasing power, and the demand for investment goods," they argued, "the rise in prices and the stimulation of buying due to the direct methods will be based on nothing more substantial than an ephemeral speculative movement likely to collapse again at any moment." (pp. 34–35)

Realizing the serious limitations of expansionary monetary

policy, the Commission recommended that the direct method, i.e., monetary policy, should be supplemented by *indirect* methods, i.e., fiscal policy. Specifically, they had in mind supplementing expansionary monetary policy with injections of new purchasing power through large-scale outlays of public capital. The only serious objection to a large program of public works had been removed, in their judgment, by the country's abandonment of the gold standard.

The Commission admitted that there had been other objections raised over the years to public works, but these were hardly serious, they argued. Among these objections were the three that (1) capital raised by public authorities merely displaces resources from private uses and cannot increase employment, (2) such expenditures are wasteful and expensive, and (3) there is not a sufficient volume of public works to give substantial employment. The Commission charged that the first of these objections, known in England as the "Treasury View," was baseless through and through. The argument that "capital raised by public authorities for construction work in depressions merely diverts resources from private industry by raising costs of building and borrowing, and therefore cannot increase employment" rested on the "fallacious assumption of an inflexible volume of credit and an inflexible supply of construction materials." (pp. 35–36)

Actually, the Report continued, there is a surplus of idle funds seeking secure investments at attractive returns during periods of depression. The problem of depression is that of the unwillingness and, still worse, the inability of private business to utilize such funds. These idle funds provided an important reserve from which funds could be drawn for financing a large-scale public works program by creating new bank credits. The deficit budgets which this policy required would raise national income eventually to levels where the budget could be balanced. "As regards their effect upon the budget," the Commission submitted, "the answer to the charge that public works expenditures throw it out of balance is that the budget can only be brought into an enduring balance if the national income is increased and this can come about only through a restoration of business activity." (p. 36) To the end of augmenting national income, in short, "public works should contribute greatly." (p. 36)

In overcoming the objection that deficit-financed public works would be wasteful, the Commission asked critics simply to recall the appalling wastage of man-power and capital equipment in depressions. In answer to the complaint that the program would be too expensive, the Commission countered that, in the absence of their program, the unemployed labor would still have to be supported out of public or private funds. The real or net cost of public works, therefore, was much less than imagined, and the community clearly received a return on its expenditures.

Finally, the Commission denied the argument that sufficiently large volumes of genuinely needed public works could not be found in depression periods. In the first place, a huge volume of public works had been suspended through the wholesale elimination of various locally and state budgeted items. There were, moreover, more ambitious and imaginative projects which could be undertaken. "Schemes for slum clearance, the erection of decent workers' dwellings, and city planning projects" offered "almost boundless opportunities in the future for construction work of the highest social utility," the Commission argued. (p. 37) They insisted that the importance apparently attached to the "self-liquidating" nature of projects by both Hoover and Roosevelt was not justified. "Since the object of such expenditures is to increase the total volume of purchasing power," the Commission members suggested, "the choice of projects should be determined by their social utility rather than by the prospect of a specific income yield accruing from the services to which the projects are devoted." (p. 37)

In brief, the Commission submitted that the goal of internal stability should be attained without undue reliance on policies of increasing (or decreasing) the money supply. Other stabilizing instruments should be used, particularly deficit-financed public spending, which would augment aggregate spending, hence production, employment, and income. All of those able to participate throughout the Commission's deliberations felt comfortable in signing the Report. This included MacIver (chairman), Angell, Barker, Clark, Gayer (executive secretary), Hansen, Johnson, Mitchell, Person, Soule, and Schumpeter.

Schumpeter wrote an important addendum, however, which is noteworthy. He stated that he wholeheartedly agreed that deficit spending on public works was indispensable to recovery from depressions, but he feared that such a policy would result in *secular* deficits. "Whilst wholeheartedly agreeing with the argument about the pivotal importance, in crises, of government expenditure on public works, and especially on direct relief for the unemployed," Schumpeter asserted, "I am disposed to lay greater stress on the necessity of not letting budgets go entirely to pieces, and of upholding the principles of careful and conscientious administration of public finances, to which it may be practically impossible to return when once the spirit of reckless expenditure has been allowed to grow up." (p. 239) Schumpeter was no doubt more conscious than the U.S. economists of postwar runaway inflations in Germany and other European countries.

International Economic Relations

Out of concern for the apparently increasing complexity of depression problems, the Social Science Research Council (SSRC) proposed in late 1933 to launch an inquiry into the elements of a unified national policy to combat the emergency. To test the timeliness of its proposal, the SSRC consulted many persons, the most notable of whom were President Roosevelt and some of his cabinet members. Roosevelt's response was altogether favorable, expressing his belief that "in making the result of [the SSRC's] studies available to the Government these commissions will be able to make a distinct contribution."[4]

Soon after the 17 November 1933 letter from President Roosevelt, the Commission of Inquiry into National Policy in International Economic Relations was appointed by the SSRC. (See Appendix A, pp. 159–60.) On 4 January 1934 the Commis-

4. *International Economic Relations*, p. 2.

sion held its first meeting. It is difficult to imagine a better sampling of opinion regarding the Depression, its problems, and its remedies. The Commission consulted public officials, businessmen, farmers, industrialists, economists, bankers, and many specialists in international affairs. It examined recent and current European and American literature. It received a large number of written statements and held hearings in Washington, New York, Chicago, Des Moines, Denver, San Francisco, Houston, and New Orleans.

The recommendations which the Hutchins Commission endorsed were segregated into political, economic, and administrative measures. Under their economic measures, the Commission argued strongly for the use of expansionary fiscal policy. "The government may enlarge purchasing power through maintaining for a time a large federal deficit, which may be created by reducing taxes as well as by increasing expenditures," the Commission suggested.[5] The Commission did not foresee that such deficits would threaten the financial structure if production and employment increased.

In prescribing large deficits, the Commission dismissed the alarm which an annually unbalanced budget aroused in certain quarters, particularly finance and industry. Far from being dangerous to the economy, the Commission argued, deficit spending was the *only* policy which held together the financial structure. As a matter of fact, the Commission warned, serious attempts to annually balance the budget would entail even larger and more enduring deficits than those prescribed, because of adverse effects on business earnings, production, and employment. Revenue was a function of income, in other words, and if incomes were not enhanced by public spending, revenue was destined to fall short of expenditures. Every effort to bring revenue into line with expenditures would further impair income, hence revenues.

The Commission went on to imply a recommendation for balancing the budget over the business cycle. It also expressed confidence that "reflation" would help to initiate recovery in

5. Ibid., p. 9.

the absence of perverse policies by industry, labor, and government itself. As production, employment, and income improved, prospects for balancing the budget would improve as well. Primarily a Commission devoted to international aspects of depression problems, much of the Hutchins Commission proceedings is irrelevant to "the new economics and the old economists." The fact that a strong recommendation for expansionary policy emerged from a series of multi-disciplinary hearings and investigations cannot be ignored easily, however.

Summary

Economic Reconstruction and *International Economic Relations* both reflect a sense of concern and commitment in the social scientists, notably economists. If there were any sympathy for deflation or wage cutting during this period, it is singularly strange that no one even gave it lip-service in a report, memorandum, or addendum. On the contrary, all evidence points to the conclusion that these Commission studies sought to redirect depression policy, to reorient it towards new goals. In both Reports, the importance of aggregate spending was recognized as the key to recovery, and the inefficacy of traditional policies to augment demand was undoubtedly accepted.

The New Economics and the Old Economists

■■ IT HAS BEEN generally recognized, of course, that no single economist ever embraced the entire theoretical framework, denoted for analytical purposes as "classical." Which is to say, there are no good *historical* examples of leading "classical" economists in the *analytical* sense. This is particularly true of American economists and their policy prescriptions. Admittedly, their strong suit was in microeconomics after the latter years of the nineteenth century, as was commonly the case throughout the profession. Nevertheless, an emerging macroeconomic reasoning was evolving along with the growing interest in and study of cyclical fluctuations.

For whatever reason, though most probably as a result of the evolving study of aggregates, leading American economists expressed no sympathy for wage reductions. Historical observations indicate their rejection of wage reductions as *a* solution to unemployment, much less *the* solution. As early as 1930 economists agreed there was no reason to believe a reduction in wages and other costs would increase employment and production. Taking into consideration the reports, the confrontations with each other and with policy makers, as well as the professional and nonprofessional literature, it is difficult to point to cases where leading American economists recommended wage reductions as a depression or unemployment policy. More often than not, it was not even arrayed among other policies for consideration, owing undoubtedly to the overwhelming consensus among leading economists regarding the inefficacy of wage policy in dealing with cyclical or chronic unemployment. In most cases, economists were even unwilling to *allow* wages to fall, out of concern that purchasing power—meaning, during this period, aggregate spending—would be impaired.

What were leading American economists recommending during the pre-Keynesian 1930s? An expansionary monetary policy was commonly suggested, but there was little confidence in an easy-money, tight-budget mix. Time and time again, economists argued that recovery could not be secured simply by making more funds available at lower interest rates. From the 1931 Harris Foundation meetings onward, evidence indicates that economists recognized the importance of augmenting aggregate spending or demand. The easy-money, tight-budget mix fell into disrespect rather early, therefore, because it enhanced only the *supply* of credit. In no small way, the inefficacy of monetary policy alone to enhance the *demand* for credit led economists to an interest in an easy-money, easy-budget mix.

Consequently, public works and deficit-financed spending won substantial support. Both a time-series and a cross-sectional approach to the study of fiscal policy prescriptions uncover various lines of reasoning, however. As the Depression years elapsed, the essence of recommended fiscal policies changed, and at any given time, economists who recommended public spending were often at odds regarding the nature of their proposals. The time-series approach reveals a more intelligible pattern: it demonstrates an evolution of stabilization policy and macroeconomic reasoning during the pre-Keynesian 1930s.

The Evolution of the "New" Economics

To digress just a bit, the financial panics and depressions prior to World War I were mere interruptions of an upward surge of employment and production. Before 1914 recovery policy, unsurprisingly, was satisfied to depend on the strong recuperative powers of the economy itself. The years between

1914 and 1929, on the other hand, were sprinkled with occasional money and banking measures designed to cope with some weaknesses in the "automatic" economic system. During these fifteen years, the Federal Reserve system succeeded significantly in mitigating the occasionally slackening rate of expansion. Professional attention centered on controlling booms with the discount rate and open-market operations. These monetary tools were intended and recognized as means of preventing "unhealthy expansion," never of preventing depression. Depression received scant attention.

Although it was widely believed in the 1920s that the Federal Reserve system had solved the problems of stability, economists' attention was devoted partially to the question of stabilizing the economy by fiscal policy. It was widely accepted during the 1920s among economists and policy makers alike that countercyclical *timing* of "normal" public works expenditures was a sufficient weapon with which instability could be fought. According to this macroeconomic reasoning about fiscal policy, increasing planned public works during depression periods and decreasing them during prosperous periods was judged sufficient to regulate effectively, hence stabilize, aggregate economic activity.

It is to be noted that this policy called for no change in total expenditures, but only for the distribution of planned expenditures in a way that spending, in particular, was stabilized. In 1923 this policy and theory were recommended and endorsed by Secretary of Commerce Herbert Hoover,[1] but it was not until 1931, however, that Congress (ironically, under President Herbert Hoover's Administration) embodied this policy and reasoning in the Federal Employment Stabilization Board. Responsible for the failure of this policy was nothing more serious than the rather naive faith that such small expenditures could stabilize the economy. During 1930, therefore, it became increasingly apparent to economists that the severity of the Depression warranted far more than mere manipulation of *normal* public expenditures.

---

1. Committee of the President's Conference on Unemployment, *Business Cycles and Unemployment*, especially p. vi.

Around 1931 recognition of the inefficacy of countercyclical timing of normal expenditures led to the idea that "emergency expenditures" would "prime the pump." This idea called for expenditures far in excess of "normal" ones. The pump-priming policy and reasoning suggested that the expenditure of several billion dollars, borrowed from the banking system, would permanently increase employment, production, and income. Once prosperity was restored, the expenditures would be tapered off. Whereas the countercyclical timing of public works did not necessarily call for deficit financing, pump-priming did, and this appears to have been the policy during the early Roosevelt years. President Roosevelt kept his 1932 New Deal promises by executing economies in the "normal" expenditures by the federal government. Simultaneously, however, in 1933–34, a pump-priming policy seems to have been followed in the form of the largest emergency public works appropriation ever passed in U.S. history.

Also around 1931 another concept emerged. In recognition of the ineptness of countercyclical timing, a policy and rationale for *compensatory spending* were advanced. This notion of public spending maintained that government should spend more and tax less in depression, spend less and tax more in boom. In other words, government should execute deficits during depressions and surpluses during booms. In contrast to the countercyclical timing or pump-priming concepts, this version accepted the fact that our economic system was subject to recurring fluctuations, and, more important, recognized that fiscal policy was a permanent aspect of economic control. Public spending was assigned the permanent task of compensating for fluctuations in the private sector. Largely under the leadership of J. M. Clark, Paul Douglas, and Jacob Viner, this policy itself evolved to embrace later the idea of varying public spending in terms of the state of private employment. The work of Clark and Douglas in 1934–35, in particular, appears to provide early evidence of the fiscal rule we now refer to as "balance the budget at full employment."

If Roosevelt's 1935 budget message and 1936 relief message were not simply politically motivated, he appears to have accepted the idea that deficit-financed government spending, far from being a temporary expedient, was essential as long as business was depressed and unemployment high. Roosevelt frankly pointed out that the level of government expenditures on public works would be determined by private enterprise. For fiscal year 1935, accordingly, his appropriation for public works was $4 billion and his deficit $4.5 billion. From 1935 on, it appears, this was the accepted policy.

To reiterate, although there was a remarkable consensus among American economists on the matter, deficit-financed public spending was recommended often out of concern for dissimilar objectives, as both time-series and cross-sectional analyses indicate. At first, economists were concerned with *recovery,* which is to say with restoring relatively full employment. Pump-priming, in particular, directed the expenditure of billions into an effort principally focused on the recovery of the capital goods industry. It was commonly recognized that reduced investment spending was the culprit in depressions, a deduction undoubtedly from the observation that heavy or durable goods industries fared worst in depressions. Public works expenditures, in short, were designed to stimulate investment-related industries.

Another mainstream argument also emerged out of the 1930–31 period. This was the idea that *stabilization* was the relevant objective of public spending. Rather than being concerned with the *recovery* of investment as was pump-priming, compensatory fiscal policy was intended to offset fluctuations in private spending.

As the years of the Depression elapsed, more and more economists converted from pump-priming to the idea of compensatory spending. By 1935 most of the leading pre-Keynesian economists solidly embraced the objective of compensatory public finance and firmly endorsed the policy as well as its reasoning. It is not clear that Keynes ever embraced the simple truths of compensatory public finance of which S. E. Harris claims him the originator. As late as mid-1934 Keynes was still a pump-primer,[2] despite the fact that the concept of compensatory public

2. Cf. Dillard, *Economics of Keynes,* p. 126.

finance had been accepted widely in the United States for several years, particularly at the University of Chicago. The evidence is that, with the writing of the *General Theory*, Keynes professed his conversion to a policy of *secular* pump-priming rather than to compensatory spending.

Historically, the macroeconomic reasoning of pre-Keynesian economists was not unlike the post-Keynesian tradition. By augmenting total "purchasing power" (which was the "classical" way of saying aggregate spending or aggregate demand), aggregate employment, output, and income would be increased. There was an output which would employ resources fully, they argued, and the task of compensatory public finance during depression was to augment purchasing power until the level of spending or demand was sufficient to clear the market of that output.

One real tragedy was that no consistent consideration was shown for tax cuts rather than spending increases as the vehicle for creating deficit budgets. Much of the opposition to deficit budgets centered on the increases in government spending which the advocates always recommended. A policy of deficit financing might have been secured had there been a tendency toward the tax-cut route.[3]

THE CHICAGO ECONOMISTS

The University of Chicago economists share an unusual position in the development of modern fiscal policy. Jacob Viner was one of the earliest modern economists to articulate the simple truths of compensatory public finance, and, from all accounts, his colleagues were similarly persuaded from the beginning and to the fullest. In 1931 Viner began to speak openly, and often thereafter, for *recovery* and *stabilization* by compensatory public spending. By 1932 he was joined by Frank Knight, Henry Simons, and the others in recommending to Washington the ideas of (1) recovery by large, continuous deficit budgets, and

3. Cf. Herbert Stein, *The Fiscal Revolution in America* (Chicago: University of Chicago Press, 1969).

(2) stabilization by balancing the budget over the business cycle. The Chicago economists continued to press for these policies throughout the pre-Keynesian years.

In 1934 Paul H. Douglas added still another twist to the Chicago theory. Undoubtedly influenced by J. M. Clark, Douglas submitted that there could be equilibrium in the output sense and at the same time, unemployment of resources. He recommended recovery by deficit budgets, as he had all along, and stabilization by balancing the budget in terms of the level of unemployment. The nature of his recommendation, therefore, was to execute deficits at levels of national income insufficient to employ resources fully, balance the budget at levels just sufficient to employ resources fully, and execute surpluses at levels more than sufficient to employ resources fully. Out of the Chicago evolution, it appears that an early statement of "balancing the budget at full employment" emerged.

It is simply misleading to submit that Knight, Simons, Viner, and their intellectual heirs at the University of Chicago have been, over the years, "consistently less enamored with Keynesian ideas and terminology than the rest of the profession."[4] This clearly overlooks the contributions which the early Chicagoans made to the development of the "new" economic policy, contributions which, by the way, are more "Keynesian" than Keynes in many ways. It also ignores the distinct likelihood that they found much of Keynes's "new" economics to be "old" hat. Confronting policy formulations similar to their own, they opted to remain loyal to the "old" terminology and ideas from which they reached the very same, if not more modern, policy implications.

"CLASSICAL" REACTION TO KEYNES

If the policy implications of the new economics were old hat to most leading pre-Keynesian economists in the United States, why were the reviews of the *General Theory* generally

4. Miller, "On the 'Chicago School,'" p. 68.

hostile? The first thing which strikes the reader of the reviews is the veritable lack of disagreement on depression policy. The challenges to the *General Theory* did not regard policy at all; they involved theory.

Among the Chicago economists, Knight, Simons, and Viner all reviewed the *General Theory*. Denying that Keynes had described classical economics accurately and that he had "revolutionized" economic theory, Knight submitted that Keynes had developed a "new system of political economy" which was conceived out of the effort to support "inflation as the cure for depression and unemployment."[5] Knight immediately admitted, however, that he was in sympathy with "Mr. Keynes's conception of inflation as the cure for depression and unemployment—with special reference to a situation in which this condition has become more or less 'stabilized,' such as Mr. Keynes's own country in and since the late 1920's."[6]

Viner similarly suggested that Keynes broke with a number of traditional modes of approach to problems, but he suspected that he broke at an even greater number. Both Knight and particularly Viner objected to Keynes's liquidity preference theory. Knight clearly preferred a *portfolio* approach to the interest rate, not unlike, by the way, modern refinements of Keynes. The things equilibrated by the interest rate were not, Knight insisted, the *desirability* of holding cash and the *quantity* of cash. On the contrary, the desirability of holding cash and the desirability of holding wealth in any other form were brought into line, Knight contended. Viner argued similarly, pointing out that Keynes completely disregarded alternatives other than cash and consols. Viner also argued that the "demand for cash for transactions purposes is, dollar for dollar, of equal influence on the rate of interest as demand for cash for hoarding purposes."[7]

5. F. H. Knight, "Unemployment: And Mr. Keynes's Revolution in Economic Theory, *Canadian Journal of Economics and Political Science*, 3 (February 1937), 123.
6. Ibid.
7. Jacob Viner, "Mr. Keynes on the Causes of Unemployment," *Quarterly Journal of Economics*, 55 (November 1936), 158–59.

Viner also went on to point out other theoretical weaknesses. For example, he argued that Keynes based increases in employment exclusively upon decreases in real wages as a result of "too unqualified an application of law-of-diminishing returns analysis."[8] Also, Viner objected to Keynes's definition of unemployment because it implied a monotonically increasing supply curve of labor.[9]

Henry Simons's review, one suspects, was not written for the consumption of economists, but it is nonetheless interesting. Simons interpreted the *General Theory* to be an argument that "our economic system has been excessively exposed and subjected to deflationary pressures," largely owing to a disparity between saving and investment.[10] On this point, Simons directly confided that he was "inclined definitely to agree."[11] Simons also agreed with Keynes in his criticism of economists for their bad application of traditional theory and their neglect of monetary problems. Simons, however, thought Keynes should have limited his criticism to the bad applications rather than including traditional theory itself in his attack, and he thought these bad applications could have been criticized "without endorsing mercantilism, autarchie, social credit, stamped money, fantastic governmental spending, the single tax, underconsumption theories and usury laws."[12] Simons concluded that many economists, including himself, would "welcome opportunity to defend Mr. Keynes against all advocates of reactionary monetary policies, and against those who think they can talk sense about our urgent economic problems while abstracting them from monetary disturbances."[13]

It might be added that Simons expressed a fear that the *General Theory* had possibilities "as the economic bible of a fascist movement."[14] In the Foreword to the German edition of the *General Theory*, Keynes himself admitted that the theory of

---

8. Ibid., p. 150.
9. Ibid., pp. 150–51.
10. Simons, "Keynes Comments on Money," p. 1017.
11. Ibid.
12. Ibid.
13. Ibid.
14. Ibid.

aggregates, which he said was the point of his book, could be much more easily adapted to the conditions of a totalitarian state [eines totalen Staates] than could "classical" theory.

Among other reviews by leading American economists, Alvin H. Hansen's was also noteworthy. Hansen interpreted the *General Theory* as a "natural evolution in the line of thought which [Keynes] has been pursuing for several years."[15] Hansen found Keynes's terminology unsatisfactory, his propensity to consume difficult to measure quantitatively, and his case for stable underemployment equilibrium to rest on the assumptions of cost rigidity and monopolistic control of supplies. Regarding the latter, Hansen commented that the "current orthodox theory—represented, for example, by Pigou—has so fully elaborated the theory of underemployment equilibrium, under conditions of cost rigidity and monopolistic control of supply, that it is only necessary here to make reference thereto."[16]

Hansen frankly foresaw a significant problem of secular unemployment, and he was pessimistic regarding its cure. Maintaining the interest rate at very low levels had already proved weak. Socially controlled investment, on the other hand, "goes far in the direction of a planned economy and might, indeed, lead straight into thorough going socialism," he warned.[17] Hansen concluded that the continued viability of a private enterprise system depended on the work of the inventor and the engineer rather than on changes in prevailing economic institutions along lines such as those advocated by Keynes. Now, it must be admitted that Hansen later underwent a *sudden conversion* to what he perceived as a new paradigm in Keynes's *General Theory*—suddenly everything "made sense" to Hansen.[18]

When these major American reviews are coupled with the others, including the British and Continental ones, it appears that the most frequent theoretical criticisms then advanced are

15. Alvin H. Hansen, "Mr. Keynes on Underemployment Equilibrium,' *Journal of Political Economy*, 44 (October 1936), 668.
16. Ibid., p. 680.
17. Ibid., p. 682.
18. For a discussion of paradigms, cf. Thomas S. Kuhn, *The Structure of Scientific Revolutions* (Chicago: University of Chicago Press, 1962).

still being made. The concept receiving the most objection was liquidity preference, largely on the grounds that Keynes assigned too much importance to it. Keynes's views on wage cutting, the multiplier, and the possibility of underemployment equilibrium were criticized in some reviews, but most of even this criticism was in the form of modification and qualification rather than rejection. Policy was seldom an issue. Taussig[19] and Hansen were not completely convinced of the beneficial effects of expansionary policy, but neither one was strongly opposed to government intervention, however. In the short run, for example, Taussig agreed that public works expenditures could prevent income from declining greatly.

Aside from the hostility motivated by theoretical considerations, there was some hostility to the *General Theory* based on policy views. Apparently, some of the leading economists who favored recovery by deficit budgets or stabilization by compensatory spending interpreted Keynes, rightly or wrongly, as advocating deficits in a *secular* sense. Keynes, of course, made no assertions regarding the inevitability of secular stagnation, but his socialization-of-investment thesis rested on the idea that private investment opportunities were declining secularly. Although developed fully by Alvin Hansen, the concept of secular stagnation pervaded Keynes's *General Theory*. It was only natural for pre-Keynesian economists to interpret Keynes as advocating a type of secular pump-priming. As Jacob Viner recently pointed out, "those who were for unbalancing the budget, 1932 on, but were critical of the *General Theory* were so on various theoretical grounds, but especially on the grounds that they interpreted it as advocating budgetary deficits as a desirable normal practice, not only for a crisis period such as the American 1933 on one, and for what seemed to them as seeing in budgetary deficits a cure-all for what ailed the economies of the western world."[20]

---

19. F. W. Taussig, "Employment and the National Dividend," *Quarterly Journal of Economics*, 51 (November 1936), 198–203.
20. Letter from Jacob Viner (14 December 1966).

THE NEW DEAL

It is well known that, during his campaign for the presidency, Roosevelt unmercifully castigated Hoover's Administration for its record of deficit budgets. Noting that Roosevelt's own second budget was an unbalanced one, however, many have given Keynes credit for the apparent change in the President's attitude. Some point not to the influence of the *General Theory* but to Keynes's interview with Roosevelt in June 1934. It is very unlikely, actually, that Keynes had any constructive influence on Roosevelt at this time. In the first place, to reiterate, Roosevelt undoubtedly regarded Keynes as a provincial Britisher who disliked and had little respect for Americans and who might try to get America to do something which ultimately would help England, not America. In the second place, Roosevelt did not understand Keynes's reasoning. If anything, it would seem, Keynes was likely to have impaired rather than improved the chances of encountering a receptive ear in Washington.

Attributing the financial aspect of the New Deal to Keynes's influence, Rexford G. Tugwell argues, is a "Keynesian myth." The former brains-trust member claims that the only truth in the Keynesian myth is that Roosevelt "behaved in what later came to be called the Keynesian manner."[21] Tugwell insists that Roosevelt arrived at "Keynesian" notions before he ever heard of Keynes, owing to "an intellectual climate created not by Keynes alone but by many others as well who were considering the same problems."[22] In short, Tugwell appears to have recognized that "Keynesian" policies had been widely accepted and commonly recommended by leading American economists since the earliest 1930s. Those in government, including Roosevelt, who behaved in what we now call the "Keynesian manner" were more likely to have been so persuaded as a result of the influence of Chicago economists, J. M. Clark, Wesley Mitchell, or any of the other leading economists whose names had long been

21. Rexford G. Tugwell, *The Democratic Roosevelt* (Garden City, N. Y.: Doubleday & Co., 1957), p. 374.
22. Ibid.

associated with what we now call Keynesian policies. For instance, Simeon Leland, one of the Chicago economists of the 1930s, has recalled:

Upon the suggestion of [Charles E.] Merriam and [Louis] Brownlow I wrote a letter or one-page memo advocating the unbalancing of the Federal budget which was sent to FDR by Brownlow—I believe through Rex Tugwell and Mrs. Roosevelt—which was instrumental in convincing the President that this had to be done. . . . Roosevelt's second budget was unbalanced and for this I think the Chicago group is to be credited, or blamed, as historians think is appropriate. Keynes contributed nothing directly to the adoption of this policy. . . .[23]

It is not altogether clear that Roosevelt ever understood the economic reasoning which underpinned the budgetary deficits he executed. Tugwell relates that Roosevelt did not understand deficits theoretically until perhaps as late as 1939, learning his theory then from M. S. Eccles. After listening to Eccles debate Harry Byrd on radio, Roosevelt telephoned Eccles to say, "You made the problem so simple that even I was able to understand it." Some others, Jacob Viner, for example, doubt that Roosevelt *ever* was motivated altogether by the new economics. Viner recalls, "From about 1935 on, the major issue in this area [budget policy] in Washington within the administration was on whether fiscal and monetary expansionism could succeed in ending unemployment, or could do so without intolerable costs, while tied in a simple and tight package with FDR's somewhat personal campaign against 'Wall Street' pursued by him not so much on economic or even on 'reform' grounds but because he believed it was a political necessity if he was to retain his 'popularity.' "[24]

The point is that Roosevelt and his advisors were likely to have been influenced by pre-Keynesian economists and perhaps even by Keynes himself, although the latter is not as willingly conceded here as elsewhere. To the extent that Roosevelt's economic policies were motivated by economic policy prescriptions rather than by reformist or political imperatives, it is quite true

23. Letter from Simeon E. Leland (26 October 1966).
24. Letter from Jacob Viner (14 December 1966).

that he behaved in a Keynesian manner. We could as easily say, however, that he behaved in a "Chicago" manner, or a "pre-Keynesian" manner, inasmuch as he behaved ultimately in a manner prescribed by leading American economists since the earliest 1930s, when even Keynes himself was not behaving altogether in a "Keynesian" manner.

The "Old" Economics and the "Old" Economists

The policy of the "new" economics and the policy of the "old" economics during the 1930s seem to have been remarkably alike. The policy prescribed by the leading pre-Keynesian, or "classical," economists in the United States did not consist of *ad hoc recovery* measures, as claimed by some. Functional relationships between employment, production, income, spending, and saving are all discernible in the old economics, and from these macroeconomic relationships, the old economists were able easily to argue against wage reductions and for expansionary monetary and fiscal policies.

The *analytical* specifications concerning Keynes and the Classics do not square well with these *historical* observations. But perhaps most of us are guilty of falsifying history because of a tendency to simplify the process of intellectual change in disciplines governed by paradigms. Rather than consisting in a series of swift transitions from less to more satisfactory paradigms, the process of development often is characterized by lengthy transition phases—periods of dilemma, search, trial, and anomaly, involving most members of the discipline. Out of these periods eventually emerges one paradigm more satisfactory than others, embodying nevertheless the interactions of many minds. The "Keynesian" policy paradigm which eventually crystallized out of the period 1930–36 represents the creativity not of a single mind but of many minds, among which one was Keynes's. ▓

Petitions, Proposals, Reports of U.S. Economists, 1930–34

1932 Report of 31 Scientific Economists

SIGNERS

Thomas N. Carver (*Harvard*)
W. N. Loucks (*Pennsylvania*)
James C. Bonbright (*Columbia*)
Paul F. Brissenden (*Columbia*)
R. M. MacIver (*Columbia*)
Merryle Stanley Rukeyser (*Columbia*)
Willard L. Thorp (*Amherst*)
George R. Taylor (*Amherst*)
William T. Foster (*Director, Pollack Foundation*)
Arthur Evans Wood (*Michigan*)
Frank H. Streightoff (*Indiana*)
Thomas S. Luck (*Indiana*)
N. J. Ware (*Wesleyan University*)
C. O. Fisher (*Wesleyan University*)
John Ise (*Kansas*)
Seba Eldridge (*Kansas*)
Arthur Gayer (*Barnard College*)

Gordon B. Hancock (*Virginia Union University*)
H. H. McCarty (*Iowa*)
LeRoy E. Bowman (*National Community Center University*)
Edwin A. Elliott (*Texas Christian University*)
David D. Vaughn (*Boston University*)
Paul H. Douglas (*Chicago*)
Everett W. Goodhue (*Dartmouth*)
Edward Berman (*Illinois*)
Phillips Bradley (*Amherst*)
C. W. Doten (*Massachusetts Institute of Technology*)
Trueman C. Gigham (*Florida*)
Walter J. Matherly (*Florida*)
John E. Brindley (*Iowa State*)
Jacob E. Le Rossignol (*Nebraska*)

1932 Telegram to President Hoover[1]

President Herbert C. Hoover
Washington, D.C.

We have the honor to transmit to you the following recommendations unanimously adopted by the group of economists whose names appear below, following a series of closed discussions on Gold and Monetary Stabilization held at the University of Chicago under the Norman Wait Harris Foundation.

QUINCY WRIGHT, Chairman
DONALD SLESINGER, Secretary

NORMAN WAIT HARRIS
MEMORIAL FOUNDATION,
THE UNIVERSITY OF CHICAGO

1. We recommend that the Federal Reserve Banks give a substantial preference in discount rates to commercial paper eligible as cover for Federal Reserve Notes. We recommend further that the Federal Reserve Act be amended to empower the Federal Reserve Board, during the present emergency, to permit in its discretion, the use of Federal Government securities on equal terms with commercial paper as cover for Federal Reserve Notes.

We recommend these measures as effective means of increasing the free gold of the Federal Reserve System and as constituting, therefore, an important defense against the consequences of gold withdrawals. We regard these measures as necessary prerequisites to the following recommendations with respect to open market operation.

2. We recommend that the Federal Reserve Banks systematically pursue open market operations with the double aim of facilitating necessary government financing and increasing the liquidity of the banking structure.

3. We urge that the Reconstruction Finance Corporation vigorously and courageously carry out those provisions of the Act which authorize it to give aid to banks by making loans on assets not eligible for rediscount with the Federal Reserve Banks.

4. We recommend that the Federal Government maintain its program of public works and public services at a level not lower than that of 1930–1931, in order not to counteract the effects of the previous recommendations.

1. 1932 Harris Foundation, *Reports of Round Tables,* pp. 413–15.

We believe that some measure of financial cooperation of the Federal Government with State and local governments is indispensable to the maintenance of adequate unemployment relief.

5. We strongly recommend the reduction or cancellation of the intergovernmental debts as an essential step toward recovery of world industry and trade, and we regard such a recovery as an important contribution to the restoration of our own prosperity. We call attention to the fact that the intergovernmental debts, while nominally unchanged since the debt settlements, have increased in real burden as a result of the fall in prices, thus impairing the capacity to pay under normal conditions.

6. We strongly recommend that the Government enter into negotiations with other countries, leading toward a reciprocal and substantial lowering of tariffs and other barriers to world trade.

Signed:

> Irving Fisher, Yale University
> Alvin H. Hansen, University of Minnesota
> Charles O. Hardy, Brookings Institution, Washington, D.C.
> Henry Schultz, University of Chicago
> Jacob Viner, University of Chicago
> John H. Williams, Harvard University
> Garfield V. Cox, University of Chicago
> Frank H. Knight, University of Chicago
> Ivan Wright, University of Illinois
> Max Handman, University of Michigan
> John H. Cover, University of Chicago
> Charles S. Tippetts, University of Buffalo
> Arthur W. Marget, University of Minnesota
> Lloyd W. Mints, University of Chicago
> Chester W. Wright, University of Chicago
> Ernest M. Patterson, University of Pennsylvania
> Harry D. Gideonse, University of Chicago
> Theodore O. Yntema, University of Chicago
> Harry A. Millis, University of Chicago
> Harold G. Moulton, Brookings Institution, Washington, D.C.
> James W. Angell, Columbia University
> Aaron Director, University of Chicago
> Chester A. Phillips, State University of Iowa
> Henry C. Simons, University of Chicago

Petition to Congress on the Wagner Bill (1930)

SIGNERS

Edith Abbott
Asher Achinstein
Emily Green Balch
Bruce Bliven
Sophinisba P. Breckenridge
Paul F. Brissenden
William Adams Brown, Jr.
Edward C. Carter
Ralph Cassady, Jr.
Waddill Catchings
Zechariah Chaffee, Jr.
Joseph P. Chamberlain
John Bates Clark
  (Pres., A.E.A., 1894–95)
John Maurice Clark
  (Pres., A.E.A., 1935)
Victor S. Clark
Joanna C. Colcord
John R. Commons
  (Pres., A.E.A., 1917)
Morris L. Cooke
Morris A. Copeland
Malcolm Cowley
Donald Cowling
Jerome Davis
Davis R. Dewey (Pres., A.E.A., 1909; Editor, *A.E.R.*, 1911–40)
Paul H. Douglas
Stephen P. Duggan
Seba Eldridge
Henry Pratt Fairchild
John M. Ferguson
Frank A. Fetter
  (Pres., A.E.A., 1926)
Edward A. Filene
Irving Fisher
Elisha M. Friedman
A. Anton Friedrich
S. Colum Gilfillan

Meredith B. Givens
Carter Goodrich
Henry F. Grady
Robert L. Hale
Walton Hamilton
Mason B. Hammond
Charles O. Hardy
Sidney Hillman
Arthur N. Holcombe
Paul T. Homan
B. W. Huebsch
Alvin S. Johnson
  (Pres., A.E.A., 1936)
H. V. Kaltenborn
Edwin W. Kemmerer
Willford I. King
Alfred Knopf
Hazel Kyrk
Harry W. Laidler
Corliss Lamont
Kenneth S. Latourette
William Leiserson
J. E. Le Rossignol
Roswell G. McCrea
Otto Tod Mallery
Harry A. Millis
  (Pres., A.E.A., 1934)
Broadus Mitchell
Harold G. Moulton
Paul M. O'Leary
Thomas I. Parkinson
S. Howard Patterson
Harold L. Reed
Father John A. Ryan
Francis B. Sayre
G. T. Schwenning
Henry R. Seager
  (Pres., A.E.A., 1922)
Thorsten Sellin

Mary K. Simkhovitch
Nahum I. Stone
Frank Tannenbaum
Frank W. Taussig
(Pres., A.E.A., 1904–5)
Ordway Tead
William Thorp
Mary Van Kleek
Oswald G. Villard

Lillian Wald
J. P. Warbasse
Colston E. Warne
Gordon S. Watkins
William O. Weyforth
Joseph H. Willits
Chase Going Woodhouse
Matthew Woll

Other Supporters of the Wagner Bill (1932)

E. F. Albertson (*Northwestern University*)
Spurgeon Bell (*Ohio State University*)
Elizabeth Brandeis (*University of Wisconsin*)
M. S. Breckenridge (*University of North Carolina*)
Paul F. Brissenden (*Columbia University*)
John B. Canning (*Stanford University*)
Frank T. Carlton (*Case School of Applied Science*)
J. M. Clark (*Columbia University*)
F. W. Clower (*State College of Washington*)
Charles W. Cobb (*Amherst College*)
W. W. Cook (*Johns Hopkins University*)
F. S. Deibler (*Northwestern University*)
Edwin D. Dickinson (*University of Michigan*)
Frank G. Dickinson (*University of Illinois*)
Henry W. Edgerton (*Cornell University*)
A. R. Ellingwood (*Northwestern University*)

Richard T. Ely (*Institute for Economic Research*)
Ralph C. Epstein (*University of Buffalo*)
Irving Fisher (*Yale University*)
Felix Frankfurter (*Harvard University*)
Leon Given (*Northwestern University*)
George G. Groat (*University of Vermont*)
Walter W. Jennings (*University of Kentucky*)
A. C. Jewett (*Carnegie Institute of Technology*)
Eliot Jones (*Stanford University*)
D. O. Kinsman (*American University*)
James W. Martin (*University of Kentucky*)
Stacy May (*Dartmouth College*)
David A. McCabe (*Princeton University*)
Royal Meeker (*Yale University*)
R. S. Meriam (*Harvard University*)
Broadus Mitchell (*Johns Hopkins University*)
W. V. Owen (*Purdue University*)
Edwin P. Patterson (*Columbia University*)

Selig Perlman *(University of Wisconsin)*

William Gorman Rice, Jr. *(University of Wisconsin)*

Francis B. Sayre *(Harvard University)*

Edwin R. A. Seligman *(Columbia University)*

H. W. Smith *(University of New Hampshire)*

Wesley A. Sturges *(Yale University)*

Arthur E. Suffern *(New York University)*

Arthur J. Todd *(Northwestern University)*

Robert H. Tucker *(Washington and Lee University)*

Francis D. Tyson *(University of Pittsburgh)*

Sam B. Warner *(Harvard University)*

Gordon S. Watkins *(University of California)*

Myron W. Watkins *(New York University)*

A. C. Whitaker *(Stanford University)*

Members of Commission on Economic Reconstruction

Robert M. MacIver, chairman *(Lieber Professor of Political Philosophy and Sociology, Barnard College, Columbia University)*

Benjamin Anderson, Jr. *(Economist, Chase National Bank, New York)*

James W. Angell *(Professor of Economics, Columbia University)*

Joseph W. Barker *(Dean, School of Engineering, Columbia University)*

Adolph A. Berle, Jr. *(Associate Professor of Law, Columbia University)*

John M. Clark *(Professor of Economics, Columbia University)*

Arthur D. Gayer, executive secretary *(Lecturer in Economics, Barnard College, Columbia University)*

Alvin H. Hansen *(Professor of Economics, University of Minnesota)*

Alvin Johnson *(Director, New School for Social Research, New York)*

Wesley C. Mitchell *(Professor of Economics, Columbia University)*

Harlow S. Person *(Director, Taylor Society, New York)*

James H. Rogers *(Sterling Professor of Political Economy, Yale University)*

Josef A. Schumpeter *(Professor of Economics, Harvard University)*

George H. Soule *(Director-at-large, National Bureau of Economic Research, New York)*

Jacob Viner *(Professor of Economics, University of Chicago)*

Leo Wolman *(Professor of Economics, Columbia University)*

Members of Commission on International Economic Relations

Robert M. Hutchins, chairman *(President, University of Chicago)*

William Tudor Gardiner, vice-chairman *(Chairman of the Board, Incorporated Investors, Boston)*

Carl L. Alsberg *(Director, Food Research Institute, Stanford University)*
Isaiah Bowman *(Director, American Geographical Society of New York and Chairman, National Research Council)*
Guy Stanton Ford *(Dean, Graduate School, University of Minnesota)*
Beardsley Ruml *(Treasurer, R. H. Macy and Company, Inc., New York)*
Alfred H. Stone *(Chairman, Mississippi State Tax Commission)*
Alvin H. Hansen, secretary to the Commission and director of research *(Professor of Economics, University of Minnesota)*

APPENDIX B

Harris Foundation Meetings

1931 Round Table Group

Mr. Charles F. Axelson, *Chicago, Illinois*

Mr. G. Frank Beer, *Toronto, Canada*

Miss Persia C. Campbell, *c/o Social Science Research Council, New York City*

Mr. Walter Case, *Case, Pomeroy and Co., New York City*

Mr. Fay W. Clower, *Chicago, Illinois*

*Professor Garfield V. Cox, *University of Chicago*

*Mr. Aaron Director, *University of Chicago*

*Professor Ellsworth Faris, *University of Chicago*

Professor Ernst Freund, *University of Chicago*

*Professor Harry D. Gideonse, *University of Chicago*

*Miss Mary B. Gilson, *New York, New York*

Mr. B. E. Goetz, *University of Chicago*

Professor Carter Goodrich, *Columbia University*

*Professor Harold F. Gosnell, *University of Chicago*

Mr. William Haber, *Michigan State College of Agriculture*

Mr. Rowland Haynes, *President's Emergency Committee on Unemployment, Department of Commerce, Washington, D. C.*

*Professor Alvin H. Hansen, *University of Minnesota*

*Mr. Haydon Harris, *Chicago, Illinois*

Professor and Mrs. Elmo P. Hohman, *Northwestern University*

Mr. W. L. Holland, *University of Michigan*

Mr. George E. Hooker, *Chicago, Illinois*

* Also members of the 1932 Harris Foundation Round Table Group.

161

Mr. Joel Hunter, *United Charities, Chicago, Illinois*

Professor Ellsworth Huntington, *Yale University*

*Miss Ruth Kellogg, *Chicago, Illinois*

Professor J. M. Keynes, *King's College, Cambridge, England*

*Professor Frank Knight, *University of Chicago*

Professor Wm. M. Leiserson, *Antioch College*

Mr. Samuel Levin, *Amalgamated Clothing Workers, Chicago, Illinois*

Mr. Walter Lichtenstein, *Chicago, Illinois*

Professor Lewis L. Lorwin, *Brookings Institution, Washington, D.C.*

Professor Robert M. Lovett, *University of Chicago*

Professor Isador Lubin, *Brookings Institution, Washington, D.C.*

Professor and Mrs. Albert H. Lybyer, *University of Illinois*

Mr. Leifur Magnusson, *Washington, D.C.*

Mr. Donald M. Marvin, *Royal Bank of Canada, Montreal, Canada*

*Professor Harry A. Millis, *University of Chicago*

*Professor Lloyd W. Mints, *University of Chicago*

Professor Royal E. Montgomery, *Cornell University*

Mr. Robert J. Myers, *Chicago, Illinois*

Professor Otto Nathan, *Reichswirtschaftministerium, Viktoriastrasse 33/34, Berlin, W. 10*

Professor Samuel H. Nerlove, *University of Chicago*

Professor D. G. Patterson, *University of Minnesota*

Professor S. Perlman, *University of Wisconsin*

Mr. E. J. Phelan, *International Labor Office, Geneva, Switzerland*

Professor Karl Pribram, *University of Frankfurt*

Mrs. Kenneth Rich, *Immigrants' Protective League, Chicago, Illinois*

Mr. E. J. Riches, *c/o Social Science Research Council, New York City*

*Mr. S. McKee Rosen, *University of Chicago*

Mr. Robin Ross, *British Consulate, Chicago, Illinois*

Professor Bernadotte E. Schmitt, *University of Chicago*

*Professor Henry Schultz, *University of Chicago*

*Mr. Frederick L. Schumann, *University of Chicago*

*Professor Henry C. Simons, *University of Chicago*

*Professor Donald Slesinger, *University of Chicago*

Professor Sumner H. Slichter, *Harvard University*

Professor T. V. Smith, *University of Chicago*

Mr. B. M. Squires, *Chicago, Illinois*

*Mr. John V. Spielmans, *Chicago, Illinois*

Mr. Eugene Staley, *University of Chicago*

*Mr. Bryce M. Stewart, *Depart-

* Also members of the 1932 Harris Foundation Round Table Group.

ment of Commerce, Washington, D.C.

*Professor Raleigh W. Stone, University of Chicago

Mr. Sterling Takeuchi, University of Chicago

Professor Robert Weidenhammer, University of Minnesota

Professor Joseph H. Willits, University of Pennsylvania

Professor Louis Wirth, University of Chicago

Professor Leo Wolman, Amalgamated Clothing Workers, New York

*Professor Chester W. Wright, University of Chicago

*Professor and Mrs. Quincy Wright, University of Chicago

*Professor Helen R. Wright, University of Chicago

*Professor Theodore O. Yntema, University of Chicago

* Also members of the 1932 Harris Foundation Round Table Group.

1932 Round Table Group

Mr. Oscar L. Altman, Chicago, Illinois

Mr. Eugene N. Anderson, University of Chicago

*Professor James W. Angell, Columbia University

Mr. Percy E. Barbour, New York City

Mr. Louis Brownlow, University of Chicago

Mr. Frederick W. Carr, THE CHRISTIAN SCIENCE MONITOR, Chicago, Illinois

Mr. Waller Carson, Milwaukee, Wisconsin

Mr. Hobart C. Chatfield-Taylor, Chicago, Illinois

Mr. Percival B. Coffin, Chicago, Illinois

*Professor J. H. Cover, University of Chicago

*Professor Garfield V. Cox, University of Chicago

Mr. Henry S. Davidson, Whiting, Indiana

*Mr. Aaron Director, University of Chicago

Professor William E. Dodd, University of Chicago

Professor Paul H. Douglas, Uni- of Chicago

Mr. Cyrus S. Eaton, Cleveland, Ohio

Professor Lionel D. Edie, Capitol Research Company, New York City

Professor Ellsworth Faris, University of Chicago

Mr. Herbert Feis, Department of State, Washington, D.C.

*Professor Irving Fisher, Yale University

Mr. Walter T. Fisher, Chicago, Illinois

Miss Hortense Friedman, University of Chicago

* Signers of the telegram to President Hoover (1932).

Miss Mary G. Gilson, *University of Chicago*

*Professor Harry D. Gideonse, *University of Chicago*

Professor Harold F. Gosnell, *University of Chicago*

Professor Gottfried Haberler, *Harvard University*

Hon. Godfrey Haggard, *British Consulate, Chicago, Illinois*

Professor Max S. Handman, *University of Michigan*

Professor Alvin H. Hansen, *University of Minnesota*

*Mr. Charles O. Hardy, *Institute of Economics, Brookings Institution, Washington, D.C.*

Professor Samuel N. Harper, *University of Chicago*

Mr. Haydon B. Harris, *Chicago, Illinois*

Mr. Carl H. Henrickson, *Chicago, Illinois*

Mr. C. W. Hoff, *Chicago, Illinois*

Professor Carl F. Huth, *Univerversity of Chicago*

Mr. Joseph Karakiz, *Chicago, Illinois*

Miss Ruth Kellogg, *University of Chicago*

Mr. John P. Kellogg, *Chicago, Illinois*

Mr. Joseph A. Kitchen, *Board of Administration, North Dakota, Executive Department, Bismarck, North Dakota*

*Professor Frank H. Knight, *University of Chicago*

Mr. Israel M. Labovitz, *Chicago, Illinois*

Professor Harold D. Lasswell, *University of Chicago*

Professor Simeon E. Leland, *University of Chicago*

Miss Marjorie Linfield, *Chicago, Illinois*

*Professor Arthur W. Marget, *University of Minnesota*

Professor Charles E. Merriam, *University of Chicago*

*Professor Harry A. Millis, *University of Chicago*

*Professor Lloyd W. Mints, *University of Chicago*

Mr. Guy Moffett, *The Spellman Fund, New York City*

Mr. J. H. Montgomery, *Manderson, Wyoming*

*Professor Harold G. Moulton, *Brookings Institution, Washington, D.C.*

*Professor Ernest M. Patterson, *University of Pennsylvania*

*Professor Chester A. Phillips, *State University of Iowa*

Mr. Stephanus J. Pretorius, *University of Chicago*

Mr. Nicolas Raffalovich, *New York City*

Professor Harold L. Reed, *Cornell University*

Mr. George Richardson, *Chicago, Illinois*

Professor James H. Rogers, *Yale University*

Mr. S. McKee Rosen, *University of Chicago*

Mr. and Mrs. Robert Ross, *British Consulate, Chicago, Illinois*

Mr. Martin A. Ryerson, *Chicago, Illinois*

*Professor Henry Schultz, *University of Chicago*

* Signers of the telegram to President Hoover (1932).

Mr. Frederick L. Schuman, *University of Chicago*

Mr. David L. Shillinglaw, *Forgan Gray and Company, Chicago, Illinois*

Dr. H. F. Simon, *German Consulate, Chicago,* Illinois

*Professor Henry C. Simons, *University of Chicago*

Professor Donald Slesinger, *University of Chicago*

Mr. Carl Snyder, *New York City*

Mr. John V. Spielmans, *Chicago, Illinois*

Mr. Eugene Staley, *University of Chicago*

Professor Raleigh W. Stone, *University of Chicago*

Mr. Edward Theiss, *c/o Social Science Research Council, New York*

*Mr. Charles S. Tippetts, *University of Buffalo*

Mr. Henry W. Toll, *Chicago, Illinois*

Mr. Robert P. Vanderpool, CHICAGO EVENING AMERICAN, *Chicago, Illinois*

*Professor Jacob Viner, *University of Chicago*

Mr. Roswell H. Whitman, *Chicago, Illinois*

*Professor John H. Williams, *Harvard University*

Professor H. Parker Willis, *Columbia University*

Mr. Henry M. Wolf, *Chicago, Illinois*

Professor Helen R. Wright, *University of Chicago*

*Professor Chester W. Wright, *University of Chicago*

*Professor Ivan Wright, *University of Illinois*

Professor Quincy Wright, *University of Chicago*

*Professor Theodore O. Yntema, *University of Chicago*

* Signers of the telegram to President Hoover (1932).

INDEX